W9-CBE-128

EASTER EVERYWHERE

EASTER
EVERYWHERE

a memoir

DARCEY STEINKE

BLOOMSBURY

This is a memoir, a work of memory,
created as truthfully as my own recollections allow.
Some names have been changed to protect the privacy of others.

Published by Bloomsbury USA, New York
Distributed to the trade by Holtzbrinck Publishers

All papers used by Bloomsbury USA are natural, recyclable
products made from wood grown in well-managed forests.
The manufacturing processes conform to the environmental
regulations of the country of origin.

LIBRARY OF CONGRESS CATALOGING-IN-PUBLICATION DATA

Steinke, Darcey.
Easter everywhere : a memoir / Darcey Steinke.—1st U.S. ed.
p. cm.
ISBN-13: 978-1-58234-530-7
ISBN-10: 1-58234-530-9
1. Steinke, Darcey. 2. Christian biography. I. Title.

BR1725.S735A3 2007
813'.54—dc22
[B]   2006031637

First U.S. Edition 2007

1 3 5 7 9 10 8 6 4 2

Typeset by Westchester Book Group
Printed in the United States of America by Quebecor World Fairfield

For my mother and my daughter

PART ONE

CHAPTER 1

ALL OF PEACE LUTHERAN's members were connected to Sylvan Beach's tourist trade. Those who didn't work at the carnival waitressed at the restaurants or worked at the gift shops that catered to the upstate New York factory workers who came to wade along Lake Oneida's muddy shoreline. In July and August, when whole families were busy frying onions at the sausage-sandwich stand or operating the Ferris wheel, my father was lucky to get a dozen people in the cottage that served as a makeshift chapel. But in winter, when snow rose to waist level and the pipes froze and the carnival shut down, and only the Sea Shell restaurant, a few bars, and the bowling alley remained open, church membership swelled to seventy and every folding chair was filled.

During those cold months laundry hung outside stiffened and the fire department came often to our house to fill up the bathtub with drinking water. In spring, mayflies clung to the side of the rectory, their black bodies so thick against the ground that for a few days the earth appeared in swarming turmoil. My father, with his blond hair, black suit, and clerical collar, seemed everywhere at once, teaching religion classes at the local elementary school, visiting the hospital and the nursing home. He often had coffee with parishioners at the Sea Shell and he bowled in the men's league. Frustrated with the shabby cottage, he persuaded a member to donate land for a real church. The congregation was too poor to bankroll a building, so he went to the synod office in New York City. The loan officer in charge of God's Bank was a tall man with a thin mustache. He congratulated my father on getting the site for free and agreed immediately to a $25,000 loan as long as my father was willing to raise the same amount from local churches.

My dad had seen a magazine advertisement for a Complete Church Packet for $17,000. He contacted Evangelical Associates Inc., and a young salesman showed up within the week in a red Triumph. He let my father drive the sports car while they discussed details for the modest A-frame. The kit included, among other things, blueprints, lumber, bricks, outlets, nails, a sink, a toilet, light fixtures, pews, a red carpet, and an altar cross. It arrived by rail in the nearby town of Oneonta. My father and other church members loaded a semi-truck and brought the materials to the site.

The crew consisted of ten congregants as well as all the drunks in town; every morning my dad gathered men from the local bars. The old carpenter in charge could not understand that the building would have no framing. It had laminated beams attached to three-inch-thick tongue-and-groove boards. By January the arches were up, but then a blizzard dumped four feet of snow and everyone stopped working.

Except for Donald. Donald was a heavyset, quiet man who worked nights as an aide at the big home for the retarded in Utica. Whenever my father drove by the building, Donald would be out in 10-degree weather hammering on the roof.

Within a month the building was enclosed and the crew came back to finish the inside. The roof was shingled, the steeple attached. My father calls that time Days of Heaven. He and Donald hauled the old bell off the cottage and attached it to the roof of the new church.

The first baptism in the new church was for four children, same mother, all with different fathers. They were fully grown so my father sprinkled water onto their foreheads. On Sunday mornings church members sang hymns and took communion. On Sunday afternoons my father took me to the carnival. I'd be fascinated to see those same parishioners changed out of their Sunday best, running the Western Shooting Gallery, the Crazy Dazy, and the Roll-O-Planes.

In winter, when the carnival was closed, they went on unemployment. The poorest families came to church irregularly, only when they had a car and money for gas. They came in loose-fitting, faded clothes. Some worked at the carnival freak show: the one-legged man with a gray beard that hung to his belt buckle and the fat lady with two children, one white and the other black. My father walked directly up to welcome these families, encouraging them to sit close to the altar. The Johnsons came most regularly. Mr. Johnson was a tall man with thinning hair and a yellowish face. His wife, who kept her coat wrapped tightly around her, only had a few teeth. They had four children, all boys. The baby had a peanut-shaped head and vacant brown eyes.

All congregations have their secret sorrows and Sylvan Beach was no exception. One was the story of an Asian woman who came regularly to church and sat in the back pew with her children. Even on the bitterest days of winter, I saw her walking along the long road to the supermarket. She owned a car, so her behavior seemed excessive and mysterious until my father learned how, three years earlier, her husband had been shot as he opened his car door. A disturbed man, a stranger, had blamed him for being denied military service in World War II. Equally intriguing was the saga of a young couple new to town. The wife was pregnant, and as her belly expanded her husband grew exotic; he wore a costume-jewelry medallion around his neck, and eyeliner and mascara around his bloodshot eyes. The week before she gave birth, she found him hanging from the light fixture in the kitchen. He wore a bra as well as a full face of makeup.

My mother was taller than my dad and voluptuous, with substantial breasts and generous hips. I loved her bare arms, the hollow of her armpits. Her face was gently freckled and her collarbone distinct and regal. When she was anxious her body trembled and her eyes darted about, unable to settle on anything solid. She was anxious a lot. Our personal phone line was also the church's, and it rang constantly with people wanting to speak to the pastor. During the day my father drove all over the county, visiting shut-ins and those sick in the hospital. Nights he had trustee or ladies' guild meetings. Saturdays he drove to Rochester to visit the home for wayward girls. My mother had packed away her pink cashmere sweater set and the jade linen evening gown, her beauty queen clothes from a few years before when she'd been Miss Albany. She preserved them in plastic in the bottom of her dresser. During her reign she'd lunched with Governor Rockefeller and had her photograph in national newspapers. The only thing she still wore from her reign was her white wool coat. The coat had an empire waist, bell sleeves, and mother-of-pearl buttons and was cut perfectly to the contours of her body. The lining was of the palest pink silk.

After my brother David was born she rarely made it out of the house and she often felt homesick. It was worst at four-thirty a.m., the time when back home in Albany she'd sit with my grandfather while he ate breakfast before he went out on his route delivering Freihofer's coffee cakes and corn muffins. Prior to their marriage, my father had promised he'd always have a hundred dollars in his pocket but now, near the end of the month, all we could afford to eat was oatmeal. Being young and unacquainted with her own temperament, my mother didn't realize how unhappy she was. She didn't understand her attraction to the knives in the drying rack, their black handles and serrated edges.

Snow banked blue on the car window as I sat in my winter jacket with the fur-edged hood, my hand on the frozen turkey beside me. My mother sat in the front seat next to my father with David on her lap. She had on red lipstick, lilac perfume, and her pale beauty queen coat. I spread my palm flat against the plastic cover that enveloped the frozen turkey. This was the first time I'd been allowed to accompany my father on a visit to bring food to poor parishioners and I knew, even at three, that it was a great honor.

Snow assaulted the windshield wipers and left a layer of talc on the glass. The station wagon moved slowly down the road, banked by evergreens, toward the Johnsons'. My father was intent on the long cone of yellow light that shone out on the glittery branches in front of us. The baby fussed and my mother settled a bottle in his mouth. The car grew quiet except for the sound of his sucking and the icy flakes hitting the metal hood with a *tink tink tink*.

The windows of the Johnson house hovered disembodied in the darkness. Their walk was a corridor of white as I followed my father up to the door. My mother held David and a small bag of canned goods: cranberry sauce, creamed corn, green beans. Even before my father knocked I heard a scurrying inside the house.

"Robert," my father said as the door flew open, "we brought you a turkey."

"Dot!" Mr. Johnson called loudly, though his wife was nearby. The little boys gathered around us, clutching slices of bread spread with jam, their jaws working diligently. The room was warm and smelled like pee and refrigerator leftovers. A bare bulb illuminated foam spilling from splits in the couch's upholstery. Nestled in a pile of dirty blankets was the sleeping baby.

My father put the turkey on the table near the woodstove and said something about the storm. Dot took cans out of the bag, staring at the labels, and set each on the table. She had the body of a teenage boy but her face was deeply lined, her features pressed into the center of her face.

"Your coat," she said, reaching out toward my mother. "I admire it." She touched the white sleeve just where the material turned over and attached to the pink lining. My mother stared down at Dot's hand, chapped red with dirty fingernails. She smiled tightly and her chin bunched. She passed David to my dad, undid the buttons, and offered her coat, the wool material draped over both her hands, to Dot.

Dot shook her head vehemently.

"Take it," my mother said. "I'm going to give it away anyway."

Dot continued to shake her head, though more slowly, and my mother pushed the coat forward, aggressively knocking the woman's arm.

"Try it on," my mother urged. "It will look good on you."

She slipped the coat over her long sweater and shapeless skirt. It hung on her shoulders and the cuffs fell to her knuckles.

"Are you sure?" Dot asked.

My mother nodded.

"I thank ye," she said.

My mother took my brother back from my father and moved toward the front door.

"Merry Christmas!" my father said to the little boys, their breath turning white in the open doorway.

On the ride back he blasted the heat and told my mother he loved her. The snow stopped and I located a star through the top part of the window. Whenever a car approached us on the highway I could see my mother's reflection in the rearview mirror.

My father had told me that God resided in everything. Birds. Stars. Snow. And most particularly, I saw now, in the features of my mother's face.

CHAPTER 2

W HEN MY MOTHER WAS nine, she began attending a Lutheran church around the corner from her family's apartment in Albany. Her parents had no interest in religion, so my mother, a quiet girl upset by her father's drinking and the arguments that ensued whenever he came home late from the pub, walked to St. Paul's and settled into a pew by herself. It was there that she would eventually meet my father, who as a minister's son held a position of honor in the congregation's insular culture.

Her own father was more interested in fishing than in God, but in earlier generations religion had consumed his family. William Miller, whose Millerite movement was a forerunner to the Seventh-Day Adventist church, was a direct ancestor. My mother's father was born in Prophet Miller's Whitehall, New York, farmhouse, not far from Ascension Rock, where ten thousand Millerites gathered on the night of October 22, 1844, to wait for Christ's return—a night forever known in church history as the Great Disappointment. Family lore has it that when William Miller returned home afterward, his wife, who had declined to join those awaiting the Second Coming, would not unlock the door for him, saying that no, it couldn't be her husband because he was with Jesus now.

My father's family was also steeped in religion. My grandfather Arthur Ferdinand Steinke was a Lutheran minister, a passionate fire-and-brimstoner. Three of his four sons became ministers, and two daughters married ministers. My father had no choice but to attend seminary. On the eve of his ordination at St. Paul's Lutheran in Albany in 1961, a year before I was born, he promised himself he'd never use the word *shit* again. He decided he was ready to be an ordained servant of the Lord, at least partly because it was the family business.

Most of my early childhood was spent in rectories: my grandfather's, my father's, or one of my uncle's. But I learned less about God inside the church walls than I did from seeing how my parents lived, how hard my mother worked in the kitchen preparing for potlucks and how my father spent almost every night at church meetings. When the phone rang in the middle of the night, as it did often, my father would pull on his black suit and clerical and head out with his Bible into the darkness.

For a while when we first moved to Connecticut my mother didn't cry as much, though I remember waking from naps and seeing that her eyes looked puffy. We moved to Zion Lutheran in Southington, Connecticut, my father's second church, when I was four because the church was larger than the one in Sylvan Beach and my father's salary, while still low, was a bit better. The church had a tall stained glass window, a patchwork of blues and golds, and an altar where my brother and I loved to play. The eternal flame, in its red glass holder, hung over our heads. My parents had taken us to Arlington to see JFK's grave and I felt the dead president's eternal flame gave importance to this one. When I woke in my bed in the little farmhouse rectory, I'd think of the light flickering inside the dark church like my heart beating inside my body.

Sometimes my brother and I would take a break from playing on the altar and go around through the sacristy door that led past the mimeograph machine where the bulletins were printed. The walls were hung with portraits of former ministers, formidable-looking men with yellow hair and heavy jowls. We'd knock on my father's office door and sit together on the leather wing chair listening to the jazz music drifting from his radio. He was supposed to be working on his sermon, the long yellow legal pads spread out before him, but he was usually reading a novel. My father was trying to quit smoking, so he kept a bar of chocolate in his bottom desk drawer, and we knew that if we sat there long enough he would give us each a square. Once we had our chocolate, he'd order us outside and we'd drift to the wooded area adjacent to the parking lot where the janitor burned old altar flowers in a metal canister. Sometimes a dying flower arrangement would be lying around and we'd loose two gladiolas and have a sword fight. Usually, though, we'd drift back toward the rectory, over the expansive lawn, to the sandbox in the backyard.

From there I could see my mother sitting at the kitchen table looking through our bills. She was pregnant again, and though Zion Lutheran was bigger than Peace, my dad made less than $5,000 a year. Still, Southington was a pretty town with a center green, and not far from New Haven, where my parents sometimes took us to Toad's Place and Louis' Lunch, student hangouts around Yale.

I was desperate to minimize my mother's sadness. I would

13

make funny faces, sing songs, and act silly to make her smile. When that didn't work, I'd ask what was wrong. She'd usually say she was lonely and missed her parents in Albany, but I knew she felt stuck with us. I'd remind her that Grandma was coming in a week. My mother cheered up when her mother visited. My grandmother was a glamorous woman with jet-black hair and hazel eyes. Though she and my grandfather didn't make much money—he drove a bakery truck and she was a physician's assistant—my grandmother was stylish: She wore a taffeta dress with a collar that rose high around her neck like a queen's cap. As a teenager my grandmother had worked as a model in Albany and even spent time in New York City, living at the Barbizon Hotel for women and working as a hat model. She didn't pretend to be interested in religion. While we were at church, she'd lie out in the yard soaking up the sun in her blue bathing suit and cat's-eye sunglasses. When she left my mother cried.

My mother wasn't always morose; sometimes we played Wiffle ball or freeze tag on the lawn, and she took us to the library and read to us every night. Even during these happier moments, through, I remember her as shaky and vulnerable. Her upper arms and collarbone were pink and tender and her face, while animated, eventually sank into a position of raw anxiety. She was a little too out-there, a little too exposed. In some ways it was a beautiful quality, like a flower growing in the yard, a morning glory or a violet, but I worried she would be crushed.

I was a scrappy little girl with a pixie haircut and ribs that stuck out of my chest, and I was as dreamy as I was ambitious. I spoke with a stutter; my throat constricted mysteriously on certain sounds and, like birdsong, I'd make a single sound repeatedly. At the time, before my stutter was stigmatized, I was just

14

another little creature in awe of the physical world. Much of my time was spent pressing my palms against the attic ceiling looking for a fenestral opening. Every day during breakfast I stared at my cup of milk repeating the word *rise*. When I'd asked where I'd come from my father told me that I, like everyone else, was a part of God. I figured I had, like God's son, magical powers. With my brother beside me, I'd pull one blanket up from the other and show him the bright sparks that popped with static electricity.

While my father was minister of the church, I was deacon of the woods, an area no larger than a square block boxed in by strips of subdivision ranch houses and the church parking lot. It was a straggly forest of scrub pines, hunched maples, automobile parts, and broken-down playpens. Garbage bags spilled old clothes and there were stacks of bald tires. In spring, white violets covered the ground and frogs laid eggs in the stream, each clump like a milky cosmos.

Here I baptized the neighborhood cats, pressing my fingers up to the soft fur just above their eyes, my fingers wet with stream water. When I'd bless them, the cats made eye contact as if they felt the tiny charge that passed between us. The dogs didn't understand the solemnity of the ritual and always licked my face. I performed weddings. At six I didn't know about the sexual aspect of marital union, but I did feel the urge to be united with another. I loved my mother, though her melancholy sometimes made our connection feel tenuous. I wanted a secure bond, I wanted to be joined for sure and forever to anything. To my first-grade teacher Ms. Truelove and to the calico blanket on my bed. Or to my best friend Mandy Messner—a five-year-old with brown bobbed hair and a precocious love of the *Encyclopædia Britannica*. I would marry anyone: Mandy Messner to her brother Greg, Greg to my brother David. The bride wore a waterlogged T-shirt as a veil and held a bouquet of withered altar flowers. I married dogs and cats, as well as a pet squirrel and a guinea pig. Life was not a requisite for marriage. I married the jungle gym to the swing set and the toaster to the blender. I made marriages that would better both parties, darkness to Popsicles and bath time to cotton candy.

Though I'd never been to one, I also performed funerals. On funeral days my brother and I waited for the hearse and watched men carry the shiny black coffin toward the church's back door. To be near a dead body was creepy and important. I'd hear my father practicing his sermon, addressing the mirror in the upstairs bathroom. His job was to reintroduce the dead to God, so he'd list off achievements—fire chief, school teacher, loving grandfather—and then assure the living that their father or sister or grandmother was even now transforming, moving into a new realm; he made the process sound like a carnival ride, a little bit scary but mostly enjoyable.

I performed funerals for a dead mouse and a baby bird that had fallen out of its nest. Once I buried a frog that my brother crushed with a rock and then tried to put back together with Band-Aids. As I said, *God, this frog was a good frog,* my brother started to cry. He felt so terrible he decided to bury his best Matchbox car, the fire engine with the tiny rubber hose, alongside the frog's remains. My brother helped me dig the hole and we squatted under the low-hanging branches of the fir tree near the driveway, decorating the fresh earth with pinecones as I said, *God, please take this frog.*

I sensed that without God, without the divine spark, the frog was just a pile of smelly flesh, but if God accepted the frog, it would be joined back into a cosmology like the ones on groovy sixties Christmas cards: bears, foxes, wolves, humans, birds, cows, all linked in concentric circles that endlessly swirled around the earth.

At the end of the summer before I started second grade, I often went to the basement to stare at the dandelion wine my father was making. Wine to me was a magical elixir and I watched the blossoms float like ghost flowers, the liquid turning from yellow to sepia and the balloons filling with fermenting gas. I was sick of using grape juice for my own communions. I figured if my father could make wine out of something as mundane as dandelions, I would use sumac berries.

I picked the fur-covered berries and dropped each into a coffee tin. Adding stream water, I stirred up the concoction with a stick. The wine was purple-black and I hid the mixture under the moldy tablecloth I used as ceremonial vestment.

The air in the evenings was getting cooler. I could almost see the frost climbing up the windows; fall would give way to winter, and as the days got colder my friends and I would be stuck inside the house. I decided to combine what I knew about communion with beauty pageants. Mandy and I stripped down to our underpants and wrapped carpet remnants around our chests like evening dresses. I found waterlogged bras in a plastic bag of old clothes. We walked along the stream snapping off cornflowers and stuck them into our hair. Greg and my brother wore scarves made from old Christmas tree lights. We all stood around the big rock in the fairy circle of trees at the forest's center. My brother found a mildewed hardback book, which he set open on the granite surface.

I began, as my father often did, with practical advice: Never put your finger into an electrical socket, and make sure to punch airholes when you're collecting fireflies. My brother, feeling uncomfortable, elbowed Greg and they both began to giggle. I heard my voice jitter as I told how my mother cried over the bananas browning on top of the refrigerator and any sad song on the radio.

I asked if anybody else wanted to say anything. The boys smiled and Mandy just shook her head. I knelt down, uncovered the coffee can, and poured the sumac wine carefully into the coffee cup I'd taken from the kitchen. I lifted the cup to Mandy's lips, then Greg's, and finally my brother David's. Each took sips that dyed the area around their mouths reddish purple. *Go in peace*, I said, as I heard Greg and Mandy's mother calling them to dinner.

By the time we made it home to the rectory, my mother had already talked to Mrs. Messner. Greg had told his mother that I forced him to drink the blood of Christ and Mandy identified the berries. Poison control suggested we all drink syrup of ipecac.

So the blood of Christ flew out of my mouth right into the toilet bowl. My father thought the whole thing was hilarious, but as the story got around the congregation I could tell that a few of the members thought my father's enthusiasm was disrespectful. Some of the older ladies looked at me as if I were a witch child holding demonic rituals in the woods.

Not long after, while my brother and I were singing songs on the altar—we'd just sung "Mr. Tambourine Man" and were halfway through Sonny and Cher's "I Got You Babe"—a bald man in a windbreaker came in and yelled at us so furiously that to this day the combination of baldness and windbreakers makes me tremble. He complained to my father and, though I could tell Dad didn't want to, he told us we could no longer play on the altar or anywhere inside the church.

* * *

With each month of her pregnancy, my mother grew more melancholy. My father had church meetings every night. She was expected to teach Sunday school and attend the ladies' guild meetings. We drank powdered milk and wore thrift-store clothes. My mother's aunts bought us our shoes. Every little loss now reminded my mother of her degraded position. When my brother and I broke the tall glass vase in the living room, my mother cried for several days, and when soda from a shaken can sprayed up on the ceiling, she acted as if our whole house were ruined.

On Saturdays I sometimes rode with my father to the apartment of a legless man who was always working on a jigsaw puzzle, tiny cardboard pieces spread over his kitchen table. Next on my father's circuit was a lady with a long gray braid who wore men's athletic socks with her slippers. No matter whom we visited, the routine was similar: After asking after their health, my father would open his traveling communion kit, a leather case with velvet grooves for the tiny chalice, a silver container of wafers, and a glass decanter. I held the chalice while he poured in the wine. I loved holding the traveling communion kit on my lap. Sometimes, if the parishioner was sleeping, my father would unscrew the top of the glass decanter, put his fingers over the top, and tip the bottle like women take a dab of perfume. The wine would make a small shiny spot on the parishioner's bottom lip. Then he'd take the communion wafer, which was about the size of a quarter, break off a small piece, and push it between the communicant's teeth. The shut-ins always wanted to hold my hand or rub my cheek, the women particularly, with their eyes soupy behind thick glasses and their housedresses with odd antiquated prints of birds and vegetables.

Phlegm blew out of the neck of a man who'd had a tracheotomy, and a lady recovering from an operation had tubes in her nose. One elderly lady, in anticipation of my father's visit, set out photos of her children in California, prepared notes on news items, and made my father and me sauerbraten with red cabbage. Before we left I held the miniature chalice while my father gave the woman the wafer. *This is the body of Christ given unto you for the redemption of sins.* I passed the silver cup to my father, red wine quivering on the bottom, and my father held the cup to the woman's lips.

Once, on the way home, I saw a man sprawled out in the middle of the street, part of his head shifted, a patch of hair flipped over, blood and mush easing out onto the asphalt. I stayed in the car as my father stood on the side of the road with the teenage girl who had hit the man. Her long dark hair lay over her white gauze top, her eyes on the man lying in the road. The police hadn't arrived yet, but another motorist had set up flares around the dead man's body.

The proximity of so much suffering made me start to suspect that God, in fact, was not infused into everything. God was hiding from me. The altar is a very different place when you only see it from the pews Sunday mornings; our rendition of "I Got You Babe" wasn't the sort of worship that was sanctified by the church. In my mother's womb I'd had tail, fins, even wings, but now any oneness with the universe was evaporating. I began to think in binaries, to divide the world into good places and bad places, heavens and hells. Heaven was the shady side of the house where the white violets grew, where I'd once seen a butterfly move inside a cocoon. Hell was the way the neighbor boy melted slugs in jars set in the sun. Heaven was my parents' bed. Hell was the garbage can under the kitchen sink. The altar, with the mysterious eternal flame and the white flowers, was the surest and most sacred of heavens; and the glassed-off cry room in back of the church, populated by dirty stuffed animals and moaning babies, was the entrance into hell.

Now that I was denied free rein in the church, the barn next to the parking lot took on the function of holy place. Bird skeletons lay over stacks of newspapers. At some earlier time the barn had been a death trap where birds flew in, got stuck, and died. Now it was more like a museum. The papers were mostly dated from the decade before, and while I could only read a little, I do remember one story about a two-hundred-year-old tortoise once owned by the king of Tonga and another about a bear who had been ejected from a sling by scientists at supersonic speed. I sat on a stack of newspapers, absently stroking the feathers of a disembodied sparrow's wing. Divinity was changing forms, the old variety rushing out of the world with an almost physical sensation, like water draining out of a bathtub.

During this period I overheard my father tell my mother how a boy at church was so anxious to see heaven that he had ridden his Big Wheel off the garage roof. This seemed to me like a reasonable solution to my own uncertainty, and I decided to follow suit. I'd drown myself in the bathtub or jump out of my bedroom window. I'd put my finger into the electrical socket, something I'd been warned against for years. I refined the details of these various plans until they took on a life of their own and began to haunt me. I became obsessed with funerals and death. Were there breathing holes in coffins? What did it really feel like to be dead?

My mother, noticing my morose fixations, told me to stay out of the barn and encouraged me to play with Mandy. Mandy was a serious girl always involved in some scientific project, collecting bugs in jars or cataloging all the leaves in the neighborhood. She was excited by space flight, *Gemini 12* in particular, and she'd explained to me about zero gravity and weightlessness. Mandy's scientific way of seeing the world comforted me, and I became so attached to her that when her other friend Georgette came over for play dates, I would stand at the edge of the Messners' yard and gaze at Mandy's bedroom window.

My father's interest was centered on race riots and the bloodshed in Vietnam, but the Messners' house took on only the happy parts of that tumultuous decade. Mrs. Messner wore bell-bottoms and a halter top while she worked on her owl macramés and Mr. Messner played his Rolling Stones records loud. Instead of going to church on Sundays, they went out on their speedboat. They celebrated Christian holidays, but without mention of Jesus. On Easter, Mandy told me the big bunny brought her six Easter baskets, and on Christmas they flew down to Florida to swim in the sea. Mrs. Messner was not as beautiful as my mother, but with her short frosted hair and cheerful demeanor she seemed free in a way that appealed to me. I began to spend a lot of time at their split-level, particularly in their kitchen, which was bright and modern.

Mandy and I, when we weren't in the woods collecting samples, would lie on her canopy bed with the eyelet spread. In school we were learning New Math. Mandy understood every concept, while to me math was impossible. She'd try to help me, explaining even and odd numbers and how numbers didn't have to be sequential to be placed in a subset. I wondered how subsets of robins would mix with subsets of Jell-O cubes, and what about that paper bag the teacher was always holding up when she was trying to explain probability? What if instead of blue or red marbles, a cupcake came out, or a butterfly? Mandy rolled her eyes and said I was pretty much hopeless.

One day we were sitting on her swing set when Mandy pointed to a tree in the yard, a big maple with a round head of lush leaves.

"That tree," she said in her most instructive voice, "has a finite number of leaves."

I looked at the tree; the leaves were lime green and there were hundreds on every branch. Inside the branches were buds, ten years of buds, maybe twenty, backed up and waiting to blossom.

"The n-number of l-leaves is infinite," I said.

Mandy looked at me. We'd been in the woods all afternoon and now our faces were red and our jackets unzipped.

"Finite," she said. "You're not even trying to understand."

I explained my idea of endless regeneration.

She shook her head vehemently.

"The leaves on that tree in my yard are finite," she repeated.

I felt a tightness inside myself. I only half believed what I was saying. There was a block in my path to the infinite and this made me argue all the more fiercely. At the end we were screaming at each other and Mrs. Messner came out, put her arm around Mandy, and told me to go home.

I ran through yards, past barbecue grills and jungle gyms, over the empty parking lot to the back of my father's church. He told me many times that God infused everything: the blue sky, the beef stew, the blanket on my bed. But what about garbage, earthworms, and the maple tree in Mandy Messner's yard? If I agreed that the number of leaves was finite instead of infinite, didn't that mean God wasn't in the tree, or in the world for that matter?

My father's office door was open, but he wasn't inside. I stood looking at the books on the shelves and the figurine of the praying hands on his desk. I circled around and opened the bottom drawer where he usually kept his chocolate, but there were just a few rubber bands and a box of the short pew pencils that parishioners used for attendance cards. I wandered out of the room and into the adjacent one with the mimeograph machine and the metal cutting board. Though I had been forbidden to do so, I opened the door that led into the sanctuary. The altar, except for the eternal flame, was dark. I moved around the pulpit to the door that led to the sacristy and flipped on the light. To move from the dark altar into the sacristy was to time travel, to move from a medieval room into a modern American kitchen, a kitchen much like the Messners' with fluorescent overhead panels, a shiny silver sink, and white Formica countertops. The silver communion cup lay mouth-down on a dishrag next to the plate that held the wafers. In the orange cabinets above the sink were rows of Manischewitz grape wine, beside them wafers in wax paper columns like Ritz crackers.

I might have not eaten a wafer if I had not found an open package, wrapped in plastic and balanced behind the faucet. I picked up the half-eaten container and stared at the white wafers. I wore a red windbreaker with a white flannel lining and navy-blue tennis shoes, my hair cropped close to my head, and I was about to taste the flesh of Christ. I unwrapped the wafers and stuck one into my mouth. It was dry and tasteless, more a marker for food than food itself, like eating paste. It was wrong, I knew, to eat a wafer before one was confirmed, but I hadn't burst into flames. So I ate another, standing next to the counter, as if I were eating my after-school snack. I thought I might get dizzy or feel my head change into a lightbulb, but I didn't feel anything, so I ate another, and then another, until the whole roll was gone. As I was reaching up to take down another packet—my plan was to eat half of those and leave them as a decoy behind the faucet—my father came into the room.

He was annoyed, or at least pretended to be. My father often seemed to be consciously evoking an emotional response rather than actually having one, and this was no exception. He marched me over to the parsonage, where he told my mother what I had done. I was told I was lucky the wafers hadn't been blessed.

I was sent to my room for the rest of the afternoon. There I lay on my bed listening to my mother's soap operas and watching raindrops hit the window, thinking of the wafers scattered around my stomach like tossed coins in the bottom of a well.

CHAPTER 3

THE ROOM IN THE hospital where our new baby brother slept was large, with a half dozen cribs and as many vaporizers spewing white tendrils of steam. Nurses sat in rocking chairs with babies wrapped in white hospital blankets. My mother got up from a rocker. Her face was gray, black circles around her eyes. Her high, tight belly had dropped and was limp and unfamiliar. The new baby had pneumonia. He coughed continuously and was having trouble breathing. He'd dropped below his birth weight, a skeleton baby with white hair that spiked straight up. I held my father's hand as we walked to the waiting room. He'd got plastic cups from the nurses' station and filled one with water. The baby had red patches of eczema around his eyes. My father held one cup under the baby's head. The water darkened the pale hair to a golden blond and splayed the strains into clumps so I could see his pink scalp underneath.

He said the baby was a child of God. He invited the holy spirit into the tiny creature's body. He made the sign of the cross on his forehead. Water trickled off my mother's chin as she took the baby from my father and held him up against her chest.

My mother stayed at the hospital to nurse the baby. On the way home my father, who usually drove casually, his wrist flung over the wheel, now clenched the steering wheel with both hands and leaned forward, glancing through the top of the windshield as if searching the sky for the tiny soul of a baby.

I was upset that my parents were so discombobulated. They seemed to have forgotten about David and me. I knew that we'd baptized the baby so that he'd be allowed into heaven but I wasn't sure if they took babies there. Were the angels willing to change diapers and warm bottles of formula? It was a good time to clarify some of my more pressing religious questions.

"Is your s-soul n-near your heart?" I asked. My father smiled that smile that meant you'd said something goofy. He didn't answer. Maybe he assumed I already knew about the nature of the soul and was just making small talk. While my mother was pregnant I was often accused of asking questions to which I already knew the answer in an effort to seem babyish and cute.

"Or is it b-by your l-lungs?"

He glanced at me. "Your soul isn't like your heart or your lungs," he said. "It's invisible."

I'd always assumed that my soul was yet another fleshy organ, less like slimy refrigerator leftovers and more like the elegant angelfish in the dentist's office fish tank. I thought of things invisible—air, breath, wind, germs—but none of these seemed substantial enough to represent a person.

"Like a g-ghost?" I was familiar, for example, with Casper.

"Not exactly." He shook his head and lapsed again into silence, his eyes watching the wet road. In the rush to the hospital, he'd forgotten his coat and his arms were goose-pimpled, pale and thin as my own.

28

My father's vulnerability connected somehow to the mysterious nature of the soul and I kept wondering, given this new information, what this essence might look like. I'd once seen a cartoon of a doughnut with wings hovering over a coffin. A girl in Sunday school had told me the soul looked like a dove. But neither of these seemed plausible now. "So it sort of f-floats around inside y-you?"

"You could say that," he answered without conviction, as if it were bad luck to talk about this now. He was silent. I was an expert at judging the malleability and meaning of silence, but this one solidified and became impenetrable. I couldn't think of anything monumental or clever enough with which to break into it, so I started saying my nighttime prayers to myself. *Now I lay me down to sleep, I pray the Lord my soul to keep.* Then I listed all the things I wanted: the sick baby to live, my mother to be happy, the Fisher-Price cash register I was hoping to get for Christmas. The list ran into silliness. I wanted animals to talk and grass to be lime-flavored candy. The rain started to come down hard and I watched the windshield wipers swing back and forth until they hypnotized me and I fell asleep.

My mother stayed at the hospital into the night. It was the first time I'd been away from her and I missed her desperately. I wanted to smell her and touch her collarbone and put my palm to her cheek. I cried as my father put me to bed and we said a prayer for the sick baby. When he left the room I decided to stay awake all night. I figured if I could stay up, the baby might live.

So I listened to the radiators shudder and watched the tiny silent airplanes swim across the black horizon. After a while I got so tired I lapsed into a waking dream. In my dream I was in the dark cry room at the back of the church, arm babies fretting on exhausted mothers' shoulders, lap babies drooling on their knees. My father's service was broadcast there through a tiny speaker hung high in the little room, set off from the sanctuary by thick soundproof glass. As my father moved around the altar, the silver chalice bright as a fragment of the sun, lilies brushed the cuff of his robe.

In the morning my father told David and me that the baby was going to live. My mother and Jonathan came home a few days later. He was still scrawny and now needed to be bottle-fed. My mother mostly slept. She'd developed an ear infection so severe the doctor assumed she would lose some hearing. Every hour she had to stick iodine-soaked Q-tips up her nose. David and I adored watching this procedure. I liked the look of Jonathan's tiny head and I was fascinated with the soft spot, so like a rotten patch of melon.

One morning my mother went back to bed after my father left in the morning and slept through the baby's crying. Now free to do what we wanted, David and I went outdoors without asking. We jumped on the beds and ate butter out of the refrigerator. At lunch my father heated up a can of soup for us and went in and tried to wake our mother. I could hear them talking in quiet voices. Then my mother's voice rose.

Once, when the baby had been crying for a while, I opened the door of her room. The curtains were drawn and my mother was wedged under the covers. I asked if she wanted me to pick up the baby.

"No, honey," she said, lifting her head. "I'll get him."

She swung her legs over the side of the bed and sat a while before standing. As she picked up Jonathan I saw that his diaper was baggy and his face purple from crying. He was still thin from being sick. Skin hung on his small skeleton and he looked like a small, sad god as she held him up against the reddish glow coming from the curtained window.

A few days later a policeman brought my mother home. He had brown hair and a barrel chest that made his blue uniform look swollen. He told my father that my mother had gotten disoriented in the grocery store, that she'd wandered up and down the aisles until a cashier had called the police. I stayed by the doorway. I had on footie pajamas and was holding Kimmie, my doll. Our father told David and me to stay on the couch in the family room and watch television. But we were transfixed by what was transpiring in the kitchen. My mother sat at the kitchen table, wearing our father's trench coat, the belt dangling down the sides of the chair. Her head was bent forward, her face hidden by her hair. The overhead light made a disk of soft silver on the top of her head that resembled a halo, and every now and then a drop of water fell from her eyes.

The next day David and I stood by the window looking out into the yard. It was early May. The huge stand of lilacs was blossoming and purple violets grew in clumps around the yard. But it was still chilly and my mother was out in her nightgown with no shoes and what looked like toothpaste smeared over her neck.

"What's she doing?" David asked.

She'd gotten frustrated trying to heat up a bottle of formula. Anything could set her off: the flush of a toilet or my father telling her there was no cottage cheese. She'd say, *I can't live like this anymore.* It was gray and windy and cold, the thin nylon swept tight against her heavy, loose breasts, and the baby began to cry again, as he had all day long in a voice raw as radio static.

We watched her walk toward my father's office. Years later my mother would describe the scene to me: She sat in the wing chair in front of my father's desk. He offered her a square of chocolate, which she waved away. All her beauty queen aspirations were gone and her life was nothing like the glamorous one she and my grandmother had dreamed about. She was desperate to let him know how bad she felt. There was a pair of scissors on the desk, the heavy metal kind with black handles, and my mother picked them up. She held them on her lap, moving them from hand to hand. *I could just stab myself with these,* she said to him. *Maybe I'll just do that.*

CHAPTER 4

A T MY GRANDFATHER'S RECTORY in Islip, Long Island, I
slept with my aunt Bonnie, who was the only one of my
father's siblings still at home. Her room held a canopy bed
with a pink bedspread. She was seventeen and had lots of
beauty routines. She put mayonnaise in her hair and believed
pillows gave you a double chin. David slept down the hall in
my uncle Alan's empty bed. Uncle Alan was away at seminary,
but he'd left his Rolling Stones posters and his corduroy bedspread.

I lay awake next to Aunt Bonnie, who often slept in curlers,
a sheen of cold cream on her face. My father told us on the
drive to Long Island that our mother was sick and needed to
rest. While she recuperated at her parents' house, we'd stay
with his parents. I wondered about my mother and prayed
with a desperation that I didn't even associate with prayer;
it was so unlike my gentle bedtime prayers or the Lord's
Prayer we recited in church. As I got sleepy my mind would
go to the photograph of the Loch Ness monster I'd seen in
the newspaper. Nessie fit in with my new theology; like God,

she showed herself rarely and her very existence was in heavy dispute.

My grandmother Steinke was raised in Flatbush, Brooklyn. She had the straightforward manner of a city girl. She was brought up Jewish but had converted to Lutheranism and was now the church secretary. In the mornings David and I would drive with her over to my grandfather's church, an austere building more like a recreation center than a traditional church. Early in the week she typed the bulletin and, later, my grandfather's sermon. When he was visiting sick parishioners she let us run up and down the hallway under the fluorescent lights, but usually we stayed in her office and lay out on the carpet coloring pictures of Jesus as the Good Shepherd surrounded by children.

In the afternoon we had run of the house while my grandmother made dresses in her sewing room. After a week I asked about my mother and was told that she was still at my other grandmother's, resting. I blamed my baby brother, whom another aunt was caring for, for her unhappiness. But I also worried that I was somehow responsible. When I tested this idea on my grandmother, she was quick to change the subject, asking what David and I wanted from the Easter bunny.

Downstairs, adjacent to the TV room, was my grandfather's office. My grandfather was a big man with lamb-chop sideburns and a rich baritone preaching voice. He'd been born in Chicago, returning to Poland with his parents when he was two before finally settling, at age five, in the States. Every wall of his office was lined with theology books and his desk was an old rolltop. He was chaplain for the fire department, and the police radio crackled like a mad oracle in his office day and night. In the closet, hung with ceremonial robes and embroidered vestments, was the shelf that held the Magic Box.

The Magic Box was made of pine with an old-fashioned brass latch. Inside were toys unlike any I'd seen in stores or advertised on television. Tiny cars with European license plates, rubber dolls dressed in fur coats with bone buttons, and net bags of blocks that assembled into Swiss villages. My grandfather insisted that the items appeared in the box spontaneously, and at that time I believed that the toys automatically replenished themselves. The box was a spot of regenerating magic like an enchanted mirror. During visits with us, when he got the box from the closet or out of the trunk of his car, we lined up youngest to oldest, and the first object we touched was the one we had to take. I heard he sometimes took the box to the hospital and that at least one child had died holding a toy from the Magic Box.

One day while my grandfather was at church, my aunt in school, and my grandmother in her sewing room, I crept into the dark office and stood in the middle of the floor watching light mutate out from the curtained window. A Celtic cross hanging on the closet door glinted, and the police radio clicked on sporadically. Static. *10-16. 10-16 at the Islip exit ramp.* Static. *10-16.* Static. *Car fifty-three on the response.* Static. *Over.* Static. I opened the closet, pushed my grandfather's robes to either side, and gently opened the lid of the Magic Box.

Inside was a fire engine, three tiny babies—two in blue diapers, a third in pink—and a plastic bottle filled with what was supposed to replicate orange juice. The stuffed monkey was bigger than the rest of the toys, the size of my hand with a blue body and a peach-colored face surrounded by white fur. There was a metal key just above his tail, and his stomach was swollen as if he'd swallowed a cereal box.

I took the monkey, closed the Magic Box, and squatted behind the dry bar in the TV room, carefully winding the key that protruded from the little thing's back. "My Funny Valentine" tinkled out of the music box and his head began to rotate, the monkey's expression dreamy, as if he'd just realized some sad thought was a little funny. Through the ceiling I heard my grandmother moving around the kitchen, so I wrapped the monkey in a washcloth and shoved him beneath the cream soda six-packs.

Every day I'd sneak down to the bar, unwrap the monkey, dress him in my doll's clothes, and feed him pebbles I got from the driveway. When I sat on the floor in the church office coloring a picture of Jesus standing in a herd of sheep, I thought of the little monkey. I liked him in a more constant way than my doll Kimmie. He was like a little God, but one I had to take care of, and this made him precious. I knew that I had trespassed, and every night as I lay next to my aunt Bonnie, I'd plan to put the monkey back into the Magic Box. In the morning I'd ask about my mother and the less information I got, the more I longed for the moment in the late afternoon when I'd hold the monkey against my chest, his metallic song ticking into my rib cage.

Years later my mother told me that after several weeks of drug therapy, her doctor started shock therapy. The white rubber band containing electrodes was wrapped tightly around her skull just above her ears and she was given an injection by a man in a white lab coat with huge hands. No one knows how shock therapy works. There are three main conjectures: that the shock stimulates the neurotransmitters, thus acting like a prolonged course of antidepressants; that the shock disrupts memory engrams, causing patients to temporarily forget their problems; and, finally, that patients see the treatment as punishment for their current behavior and stop acting depressed. All I know of shock therapy I know from movies: a jolt of electricity convulses the body, muscles jerk. I imagine my mother's legs vibrating under the leather straps and her eyes rolling back.

On Ash Wednesday, people kneeled at the communion rail as my grandfather rubbed ashes into each person's forehead. *From dust you came and to dust you shall return.* On Good Friday the crosses were shrouded in black velvet and my grandfather read the Passion while David and I sat with my grandmother in the front row of metal folding chairs, eating candy out of her purse. Because the room was more like a gym than a sanctuary I felt sorry for my grandfather. The informality of the setting made it seem as if he was playacting.

Mostly I thought about the monkey, whose ceremonial meaning was in perfect relation to his being. I now attributed to the monkey a tremendous range of emotion. The pebbles gave way to tiny chunks of food I stored in a napkin from my lunches and dinners. I felt sorry that the monkey could not speak and so had to rely on communicating by the sad song playing out of his belly. It had been weeks since I'd stolen him and I assumed my grandfather was too busy to keep track of all the toys in his Magic Box.

The day before Easter I was dyeing eggs with my grandmother and aunt at the kitchen table, which was covered with newspapers, hard-boiled eggs sitting in cups of dye. My grandfather came up from his office, where he'd been working on his Easter sermon. He wore his black pants and a white T-shirt, golden auras of sweat under each arm. He asked if my brother and I had been in his closet. A lump of blood thumped out of my heart and I stared into the cup of purple dye where an egg was taking on a lavender hue.

"Follow me, children," he said, leading us down the stairs to the TV room where he settled his girth onto the colonial couch and asked again if we'd been in his closet. Both David and I shook our heads.

"Darcey," he said, motioning to me.

I knew what was coming so I walked over and bent across his knees. He smelled of Old Spice and sweat. I could feel his kneecaps against my ribs and see the covered bridges on the couch's upholstery and below that his yellow toenails. I heard David cry out and the sting on my bottom simultaneously. My brother hung back from his grip, screaming.

Afterward David and I went out in the yard and sat gingerly on the rusty swing set.

"Now the Easter bunny won't come," David said. He had on corduroy pants and red Keds tennis shoes. Every time he moved past the metal frame he hit the pole with a stick. The tiny thrump vibrated through the metal, a sound pleasing to both of us.

The next day we got up in the dark and my grandmother dressed us in matching outfits, a blue jumper with white tights for me and blue short pants and a blazer for David. We were told our grandfather was already at church and that the Easter bunny would come while we were at the sunrise service.

In half light we sat on folding chairs set up on the lawn facing the church's front doors. After a while the door flew open and my grandfather, his fur-collared black cape swinging out from his white vestments, strode out to the wooden lectern. The cape was fastened with a black grosgrain ribbon and he wore a slouchy Martin Luther cap.

"He has risen!" he bellowed.

The assembled people stood and shouted. "He has risen indeed!"

I was worried about the fate of my monkey as I listened to the story of the ladies coming to search for Jesus and finding the angel sitting on the rock. I must have heard the story before, but this time something about the angel sitting above the women made me think of a guy with a New York accent eating peanuts. I thought the whole setup was very funny. The ladies came looking for a dead body but found a stand-up comedian instead. When we got back to the rectory, my aunt Bonnie gave us each a piece of colored cellophane matching the cellophane in our baskets. Then they let us loose to search. Mine was hidden behind the couch in the living room. Though I felt grateful that my aunt had let the Easter bunny know we moved locations, the marshmallow chicks and chocolate seemed unimportant compared to my monkey.

While my grandmother and aunt scored the ham and used cloves to attach circles of pineapple, I snuck down to the bar, crouched beside the column of cream soda, unwrapped the monkey, and gave him a chip off my chocolate rabbit. I looked at his delicate features arranged in a sleepy expression. My heart felt as if it had fallen through my stomach and turned to metal like the monkey's. I pulled off the little pink dress, untied the ribbon around his head, and crept down the hallway to my grandfather's office. The closet door was open and I lifted the lid of the Magic Box. One of the babies was left, alongside a net bag of plastic minnows and a red yo-yo. I kissed the monkey on the forehead and placed him back inside the box.

After the eleven o'clock service, my aunts and uncles came over and we ate ham and macaroni salad. I asked every half hour if my father was coming and I was told each time that he was late because of his own church services and traffic on the Long Island Expressway. After a while I heard a sound in the hallway and there he was in his black suit, his hair newly cut. We ran to him and hung on his neck.

"I have a surprise for you," my father told us, turning and pointing to my mother, who stood shyly behind him.

In the three weeks since we'd seen her, she'd lost weight. Her arms were thinner and her face narrow. She wore a sleeveless brown dress, white gloves, and a small white hat. She hung back, embarrassed, but my father took her hand and pulled her into the room. There was a hush as she stood there looking down at her high-heeled shoes. At first she seemed bewildered but then she smiled, her eyes filled up with water, and she kneeled beside us. From her purse she gave us each little bags of jelly beans. Taking my baby brother from my grandmother, my father kissed him on the forehead and passed him to my mom. My grandfather told us to show our Easter baskets to our parents. When I pulled out mine I saw that the monkey sat between the headless chocolate rabbit and a row of marshmallow chicks.

CHAPTER 5

A FTER HER BREAKDOWN MY mother quit the ladies'
guild and sometimes even missed Sunday services. I heard
several parishioners ask my father if Mrs. Steinke was still
sick. At first I was happy to be back in our rectory, where my
mother cared conscientiously for Jonathan, changing his diapers and heating his formula. No one talked about what had
happened. I watched her moving around the kitchen and
making the beds upstairs. If she spent too long in the bathtub
or out shopping I'd feel my heart race.

Money became more of an issue. At the end of the month
she ransacked my father's pockets for change so she could buy
diapers. The church council, which consisted mostly of Ger-
man immigrants who worked as machinists, had agreed to up
my father's salary to $5,400 a year. The rectory was rent-free
and when we first moved in parishioners had brought over
groceries and casseroles, but the longer we were there the
more charity diminished. My father informed the trustees
that if they weren't going to pay him more, he'd have to take a

second job. Though they grumbled, he began substitute teaching several days a week at the local high school.

When my father took twenty-five dollars for performing a funeral, the trustees summoned him for an emergency meeting. He was reprimanded and told that he had to give the money back. He refused, explaining that the deceased had not been a church member. The tension in church was like a force field. I was still up at night but now, rather than trying to read the theological journals in my father's bathroom, I would creep down to the middle stairs and listen to my parents.

One night their argument was fiercer than usual. My mother, while looking for something in my father's desk, had found several unpaid bills.

"I can't live like this," she said.

"We'll pay them," he said.

"I won't live like this," my mother said. "The kids in shabby clothes. I'm ashamed to be seen in the supermarket."

"What can I do?"

"It's not right," she screamed, and started to cry.

After that my father would try to appease her, saying it wouldn't always be like this; eventually he'd make a better salary. My father was beginning to wonder if the church was the place he wanted to spend the rest of his working life. He'd gotten a master's degree from Wesleyan and interviewed for a job teaching English at Exeter. Now he was considering clinical pastoral education to become a chaplain.

I sat on the steps listening, my heart hitching up and balancing on every word my mother said. During this time school was harder for me. My stutter had gotten worse and I had trouble reading passages out loud. When asked to read an article from the *Weekly Reader* about stewardesses, my vocal cords constricted and I'd stammered so violently that my face got red and my teacher asked me to stop. I also had glasses for my lazy eye. I had to wear a black eye patch around the house as I preformed corrective exercises like filling in all the *a*'s on a sheet of newspaper and lying on the floor watching the tennis ball my mother swung on a string over my head. These exercises so exhausted my lazy eye that at night, once the patch was off, my eye moved sluggishly around to various objects in my bedroom.

During the day David and I tortured our little brother, Jonathan. We'd give him an olive saying it was a grape. Or shake pears down from a tree over his mosquito-netting-draped carriage. The pears would weigh the netting down around his face and he'd scream.

It was only in Sunday school that I enjoyed undeniable prestige. Not only was I the minister's daughter, but I'd distinguished myself by memorizing Bible verses and being the quickest to answer Old Testament questions. Where was Moses found? *A basket!* Who was Abraham's wife? *Sarah!* I screamed, while the other kids sat bored and sleepy on their folding chairs around the long Sunday school table.

Christmas that year was a great relief. Rather than worship a spooky Jesus who hung on a cross, I got to meditate on a tiny infant no bigger than one of my dolls. I loved that I was older than baby Jesus and so could have some authority over him. This feeling of mastery helped me. Sometimes I'd pretend my baby brother was baby Jesus and creep into his room at night to see if he radiated light, but his only magic was a toothless smile that sent both my parents into a state of euphoria. At the same time I had been trying to put the neighborhood cats into a trance and to get the rabbit in the yard to come up to me. I was also impressed that baby Jesus had induced animals to stand quietly and watch him sleep: sheep, horses, those fascinating and exotic two-humped camels. Above all else this convinced me that my baby brother was in possession of the godhead.

The Christmas before, much to my dismay, my doll Kimmie had played the part of baby Jesus in the children's nativity. Kimmie is a girl, I thought indignantly as I sat with my mother in the front row and watched the dark-haired Mary pick up my doll and show her reverently to Joseph. But finally I'd come to realize that it was an honor, as my father was always insisting, for my doll to play the little Lord.

So as we lit the purple candles in the pine-needle wreath and opened the little cardboard windows of the advent calendar, I began to give baby Jesus lessons to Kimmie. I taught her how to look like a boy, how to say "Mary" and "Joseph," and how not to cry when the angels came down. Efforts to get her to sing "Silent Night" and glow in the dark, however, were unsuccessful. Mostly baby Jesus was sort of lazy. Just like my little brother, all he wanted to do was sleep in my toy cradle nestled in the crumpled paper I'd colored yellow to look like straw.

When the big night came, I stood in the pulpit wrapped in a bedsheet gown, with cardboard wings covered in tinfoil attached to my back and a clothes-hanger halo, looking down into a manger filled with real straw. I saw Kimmie's natty blonde bangs. Just that morning I'd sheared the synthetic threads off with scissors so everyone could see the blue lines I'd drawn with Magic Marker around her eyes.

My father read the Christmas story from Luke, and while the congregation sang "What Child Is This?" I tried to figure out what it would be like inside the baby brain of God. As I tried to get my thoughts around the zillion particles of light swirling around in a whirlwind, I felt time wobble sideways and got so dizzy looking down into the manger that I had to lean against the rail of the pulpit for support.

A new year came and another Easter approached. At night my mother still said bedtime prayers with my brother and me, but on Good Friday she stayed home with my baby brother. David and I walked alone across the yard, wind stinging the tips of our ears. Inside the church all the crosses were draped with dark velvet and the altar was dim, lit exclusively by the red eternal flame.

My father came through the doorway to the altar, opened his Bible, and began to read the Passion. He stood in the dark in his long black robe, the big cross behind him draped in black. His hands on the pages of the Bible glowed white as he read about the place of the skull, about the water and red blood gushing from the slit in Jesus's side, how gray clouds pressed so tightly into the heavens that darkness fell over all the earth. I hadn't realized that Jesus after the crucifixion was as dead as the frog my little brother had crushed into pieces, but that Jesus had thrown off death like a flu bug. I figured God must have told him to hold a penny under his tongue or to concentrate as hard as he could on his own heartbeat. The trick probably required commitment: a cool bath every evening for several years accompanied by imagining oneself as the spoor of a dandelion.

Making the sign of the cross, my father walked to the door at the back of the altar, opened it, and was gone. I pulled David down the stairs into the church basement where we played with the Fisher-Price airport in the nursery. I ran the plastic plane across the runway while my brother landed his tiny helicopter on the roof. After my father had taken off his robes, he came down to turn off the basement lights, then the ones in the sanctuary and the narthex. We stood beside him as he extinguished the light in the hallway and we walked together across the lawn back to the house.

Randall Scott Fletcher. James Gerald Flynn. A balding, stocky man in a white clerical collar and black short-sleeved shirt stood in the rain in the middle of a knot of people at the post office in Southington, reading the names of the Vietnam dead. *Gerald Henry Forgue. Daniel William Foster.* A college girl with long, straight hair and granny glasses held a black umbrella over the clergyman's head. The minister was a bit older than my father and he read nervously but reverently, as if reciting the Lord's Prayer. The crowd was diverse: ministers with tentative sideburns, girls in gauze dresses, gray-haired church ladies with OUT NOW buttons pinned to their sweaters. I leaned into my father's pant leg as rain dripped off our umbrella down in a circle around us. On television I'd seen napalm explode, expanding over one thatched hut after another, and though my parents rushed to snap off the TV set, I'd seen enough to get a sick feeling in my stomach. I didn't fully understand what was going on in this wet, oil-streaked parking lot, but I understood it was as important as anything that went on inside our church's walls, and I understood that my dad was trying to do his part to help stop what was happening in Vietnam. "God is on the move," my dad liked to say.

Visiting the sick and carting turkeys to poor people at Christmas wasn't enough for him anymore. Now he cajoled his blue-collar flock to share its modest suburban swatches of green with inner-city kids through the *New York Times'* summer Fresh Air Fund. He urged the white parishioners to volunteer at a breakfast program in New Haven run by the Black Panthers. He put up yard signs and worked as a poll runner for a Democratic antiwar candidate. Sometimes it seemed that as my dad threw himself into saving other families, into trying to fix the world, he had little time for mending the cracks in his own family. But it was also exciting to be swept along as a tiny bystander as he immersed himself in social changes that most people experienced only by watching the television news.

Nearly every Friday night we drove to Zion New Haven for what was known, impishly, as LSD: Liturgy, Supper, and Drinks. The event was run by Ray Schultze, a friend of my father's from seminary. Reverend Schultze was a tall, thin, charismatic man who'd married the former secretary to theologian Jaroslav Pelikan; together he and his wife, Margaret, were one of the power couples of the Lutheran intelligentsia. The congregation had built a rectory out in the suburbs, but Reverend Schultze refused to live there. He wanted to live in the old parsonage, a row house next to the church in a poor section of the city. The parsonage was both grand and run-down, with a mantel carved with pineapples, and buckets in the hallway that caught the rainwater that seeped through the roof. The doors were always unlocked and a bedroom on the first floor was open to anyone who needed a spot for the night.

The Friday-night gatherings brought together Black Panthers, seminary professors, Korean missionaries, and members of Valparaiso University's Prince of Peace Corps who had come all the way from Indiana to do political organizing. David and I tore around the house, playing hide-and-seek with black kids from Zion and ministers' kids whose parents had been missionaries in Africa. These gatherings left my dad euphoric. My mom, on the other hand, didn't trust the Black Panthers or the flower-child types, and she kept a close eye on my brother and me. She'd grown up in a kind of ghetto herself, and there was nothing groovy to her about poverty and urban decay. She'd started going to my grandfather's church not so much to spiritually liberate herself from the dreariness of her dad's drinking or her mother's struggle, but to seek refuge from them. If for my dad religion was about forward motion, for my mom it had all been about safety and stability. She'd been taught to follow rules, not to make waves. Later she told me that while she kept her mouth shut during Zion's LSD parties, on the way home in the car she'd often think to herself: *All these liberals—if they really knew what the ghetto was like, they wouldn't want anything to do with it.*

Our last Christmas at Zion my father organized a birthday party for baby Jesus in the church basement. He taped streamers to the ceiling and everyone was given a party hat and a tiny plastic trumpet. He gathered us children into a line for pin the tail on the donkey. The winner received a glow-in-the-dark cross. The organist played Sunday school songs on the piano until it was time for cake. Lights were extinguished and we all sang "Happy Birthday" to the little Lord.

When the song was over and the lights came up, the head of the trustees, a short man with a comb-over, stood beside my father holding a half dozen white balloons; he told the gathered members that these were my father's Christmas gift. Inside the milky latex, I saw the green bills I knew we needed to buy Christmas presents.

Members of the ladies' guild cut up the birthday cake and my dad delivered slices to the elderly people from the nursing home. After everyone left, we pulled down the streamers and set out the trash. My mother had already taken Jonathan back to the parsonage, so my father got David and me into our peacoats and told us to hold hands as we crossed the icy parking lot.

It was dark outside, the snow shiny and the wind numbing my face. The balloons beat against one another with tribal urgency. Wind cracked branches and blew up snow and the balloons caught in the wind stretched out like dogs on a leash. One of the cash-laden balloons got loose, drifting over the sandbox and up into a pine tree. My father ran after it, across the yard and into the woods.

PART TWO

CHAPTER 6

THE FIRST PLACE WE moved once my father left the parish ministry was Norwich, Connecticut. Norwich was a military town, and we lived in a low-income development of duplexes. Parish life seemed lush and poetic compared to our new life as members of secular society. Every day the school bus dropped us off at the center of our apartment complex and, along with dozens of other children, we dispersed into rows of identical brick houses. Our basement door was left unlocked and we'd wait for our mother to get home from her job at the department store. In the early fall, when the weather was warm, my brothers and I ran in the woods adjacent to our row of condominiums. These woods were not as hospitable as the ones in Southington; the stream water gave us sore throats, and each of us found ticks burrowed into the flesh of our stomachs. As the weather got cooler we lay in the basement playing checkers, our pet mouse crawling around on our sweaters.

Though we weren't supposed to have visitors after school, sometimes neighborhood kids came to the back door. Many were children of people who worked at the local mall; a few had dads still in Vietnam. One girl, with a bowl haircut and gray allergy circles under her eyes, talked incessantly about guns, AK-47s and the pistol her father strapped to his ankle in case he was taken off guard by a "gook."

Tommy stopped in several times a week. He was a fifth grader with black hair and large dark eyes squinted in ridicule. His body was thin but strong; I once saw him carry concrete blocks into the woods from the building site at the end of our row of condos. Tommy's father was a policeman, a heavyset guy with a thing against seat belts. Everyone in the neighborhood knew how he'd seen a boy burn to death, trapped in a car by his seat belt. Tommy spent hours denigrating safety in general and seat belts particularly. When this subject lost its interest for him, he'd tease me.

"D-Darcey, b-beeen able to t-talk l-lately?" Tommy said, stuttering only on the letters that actually gave me trouble.

My father told me that the schizophrenics at Norwich State Hospital for the Mentally Insane, where he worked that first year he left the parish, were quite theologically engaged. Ralph, my father's favorite, came into his office every day and while making small talk—Was God located in the washcloth? In the bathwater? In the Salisbury steak?—he'd steal pencils. Ralph then went next door to one of the social workers and sold the pencils for ten cents apiece. He'd go on like this, stealing pencils and selling them, until late in the afternoon when he finally had enough money for a pack of cigarettes.

Early in the year I began to develop boils. Our pediatrician said that my father had brought home a staph infection from the hospital, and while we'd all been exposed, I was the only one who manifested the infection. When a boil developed my skin stretched, grew warm, and a hard sore pushed up, the core often as large as a small corn kernel. On these days I stayed home from school, my mother took a day off, and I helped her with housework. While soap operas played on the television we'd sit on the couch and fold laundry. My mother spoke to me about how as a little girl she'd told the landlady, while my grandmother hid, that they did not have the rent money. Every night she got my grandfather from the local bar. *Just one more*, he'd say, inviting her onto the stool beside him to drink a cherry Coke.

Her voice got grainy as she again told me how at nine years old she'd gone into my grandfather's Lutheran church and sat in the pew every Sunday all by herself. Other stories centered on her father's unfaithfulness, my father's immaturity, her own wasted potential. All became ritualized until I felt a patch of grayness, viral and unresolved, passing from my mother into myself. When she carried the laundry downstairs I looked in the mirror that hung over the couch. Though I no longer rode along with my father to visit shut-ins, I felt when I had a boil I was helping him with his work. The boil was incongruent with my features, like a patch of insanity. Boils gave me special powers. It was only when I had one that my mother relayed to me her sorrow.

I had tried collecting African violets and empty perfume bottles, drying flowers in the pages of my books. But none of these gave me the holy feeling I'd sometimes had in Southington. A small contemporary statue of Mary stood on the coffee table and there was a painting of a cross entwined with Easter lilies over the couch, but neither meant much to me. I was more interested in my mother's beauty queen clothes wrapped in plastic at the bottom of her dresser.

One day when I was home with a boil my mother called me into her bedroom. An aqua dress with a taffeta skirt lay out on the bedspread. I touched the smooth material of the satin sleeve and fingered the tiny wrist button.

"It's for you," my mother said.

I could not have been more pleased if my father had given me his traveling communion kit. Many of my childhood fantasies centered around wearing my mother's Tulip Queen gown as I acted out the motions of the communion ritual. I put the dress on and pretended to skate around the room, my bare feet gliding over the shag carpet. The next day after school I slipped the dress on over my jeans, zipped my winter coat up over the bodice, and ran to the hill in back of our duplex.

I tried running with my arms up. I tried running on my tiptoes. I tried tipping my head down and running kamikaze style. I tried running with my hood up. I tried running with my hood down. I tried to flap my arms. I tried to pray to God to let me fly. I tried to beg God. Nothing worked. I looked down at the netting bulging from under my winter coat.

I climbed back up the hill and went into the woods. Inside the tree line I saw a pile of magazines. On the covers were women with hair like lions' manes and breasts spilling out the sides of their bikini tops. When I opened one I saw a woman with flawless skin, her head thrown back, mouth open. Another magazine showed a woman wearing only a cowboy hat, and in another a girl lay on a pink fur bedspread. My favorite photograph was of a man and woman entwined in the middle of a green lawn.

Each day after school I went directly to the base of the tree where I'd hidden the magazines. Children before me had found books with special powers, and I knew that the women's ecstatic expressions were like magic spells. One day as I approached

I saw Tommy sitting in my spot. He had his back to me, his knees tucked under him in an almost girlish position, his head lowered as he turned the pages reverently. He looked unlike his sullen self and more like a boy in a library.

My first impulse was to creep out of the woods. Tommy had enough on me already. I was repeating third grade and besides my stutter, I couldn't remember the direction of certain letters and had to sit in the cloakroom and run my finger over sandpaper *b*'s and *d*'s for several hours each day. But I also felt proprietary about the magazines. I didn't want him to move them to his tree fort.

"Hey," I said to him.

He swung around. "Get out of here!" he yelled. "This isn't girl stuff."

"They're g-girls," I said.

"Whores!" It was clear he adored the word. He smiled, hugging the magazine to his chest.

I reached down and picked up one with a woman in a leather bikini on the cover. It was heavy, waterlogged, the pages flipped open to a photograph of a man with long hair sucking the nipple of a woman with a dreamy expression on her face. I thought Tommy would denigrate the picture and tease me, say something about my swollen eye or make fun of my stutter, but like an icon, the image quieted him.

"I bet they don't w-wear s-seat belts," I finally said to him, motioning to the couple.

All he could do was shake his head.

CHAPTER 7

T HAT SUMMER WE PACKED everything into a U-Haul and my father drove the truck behind our station wagon through the Appalachian Mountains toward Harlan, Kentucky. At night we'd stay in cheap motels, my brothers and me in one bed and my mom and dad in the other. All had televisions on Formica dressers and carpets pockmarked with cigarette burns. They had copper-colored plastic ice buckets, shiny metal ice machines, and mossy smells that, as we drove deeper into the mountains, turned into the scent of fermented earth.

During the day we rode with my mom on roads so curvy we'd be thrown from side to side in the backseat. We'd exaggerate this sensation by screaming until my mother reached back and slapped at us. She wore Jackie O sunglasses and a silk scarf over her hair, a jean skirt, and a cotton tunic. Even twenty pounds overweight my mother was still beautiful, delicate and glamorous as a celebrity recently released from rehab.

About halfway through the trip, after a gas station lunch of corn dogs and RC Cola, I got to ride with my dad. I had the whole passenger seat to myself and I could look down at my brothers hanging their feet out the back window of the station wagon in front of us. My dad's face was set in an amused expression. He often seemed to find his own life odd and fantastic. Beside me was a shoe box containing my perfume-bottle collection, and as I unwrapped each to make sure the glass hadn't cracked, I stole glances at my dad. He drove with a sort of languid preoccupation.

"Ha-lan Ken-tuc-kee!" he said, looking over at me. "Do you know how those coal miners have suffered?"

I did only because he'd told me a hundred times. Ever since he'd accepted the job, he was fixated on Father O'Malley, a well-known Catholic priest who worked in Harlan with the poor miners—simple-hearted men, many of whom were dying in the Harlan hospital of black lung. He'd told me how they worked long hours underground with just a carbide lantern. How they lived in coal camps without electricity or running water.

Now, instead of ministering to people who were convinced they were space aliens or reincarnations of Julius Caesar, my father would go underground. Down deep into the mine shaft, wearing his black suit and clerical and carrying the traveling communion kit. He'd pray with the miners, their faces smudged with coal dust, the beam of light on their helmets illuminating the white wafers on the tiny silver plate.

"The miners are treated like animals by the owners," my father said. "Some live in shacks with no bathrooms."

"Why don't they w-work someplace e-else?"

"They can't," my father said. "Coal mining is all they know and when they strike, the owners send in goons to beat them up."

"That's b-bad," I said, kicking under the dashboard. I knew that if I didn't interrupt my father soon, he'd bring up gory details of miners hooked up to oxygen tanks.

"What about our s-school?" I asked. "What is our s-school like?"

"School?" my dad asked.

"What d-does it l-look l-like?" He glanced at me and I could tell he hadn't seen the school on his earlier weekend visit to Harlan. He had no idea what school we would go to. He wasn't even sure Harlan had a school. All he knew was that Harlan had a hospital where miners with blackened lungs wore oxygen masks and where, soon, he'd be moving bed to bed, telling them God was on their side.

"Let's listen to the radio," he said. "I'm taking a shine to this country music."

Merle Haggard's voice filled up the cab and my father took the curve in the road with leisure. Everything I'd heard about God was true of my father. He was both loving and aloof. He asked people, people like Noah, to do impossible, idiotic things, like packing up everything and driving into the wilderness.

That night my mother called David and me into the motel bathroom. Jonathan, who was five, lay naked and facedown over her knees. She had just bathed him in the tub with the moldy shower curtain. Jonathan's white eyebrows and hair were pale as a polar bear's fur under the overhead light, and strands fell toward the floor as if he were being electrocuted. He struggled but my mother held his body firmly. She'd taken off her sunglasses but her dark hair was still held back with the floral scarf tied at the base of her neck.

"Come," she said, motioning us forward with her free hand.

David and I stood beside Jonathan's body. He complained

bitterly. *Let me up! Stop it!* But my mother ignored him; she was mesmerized by his bare butt.

"Do you see it?" She pointed with her finger at what looked like a tiny white thread stuck to one of his butt cheeks. The little worm lifted its head and swung around in a desperate effort to get back inside its dark place of rest.

The rims of Father O'Malley's glasses were fixed with Scotch tape and his face was flushed purple. When we'd arrived at the Harlan hospital he'd seemed not to remember he'd promised my father to find us a place to live. After a few phone calls, while my brothers and I got candy bars out of the vending machine, he returned to tell us about Caterine's Creek.

Though it was a sunny afternoon, vines draped from the trees made it seem like twilight. I held on to the rickety rope and walked over the plank bridge. Below in the ravine lay a burned-out car and a screenless television. The trailer stood with a half dozen others, beige and slanted like a dog on its knees. Inside the place smelled of cigarette smoke, and moldy towels filled the kitchen sink.

"I'm relieved," Father O'Malley said. "I thought this place might be uninhabitable." He smiled at us, a congenial if slightly unhinged grin, and was back out the door telling my father he'd see him first thing Monday morning.

My mother collapsed against the sink and our father sent us outside. There we examined the red dirt underneath the trailer. With a stick, I dug up clumps and spread the mud over the backs of my hands. I picked through the pile of glass bottles in back of the trailer, separating out pickle jars from soda bottles. Every now and then I heard my mother's voice rise up. *No money. Completely destitute. Last straw.* All the other trailers appeared vacant except the one at the far end, which had white curtains in the windows and tomato plants surrounded by a chicken wire fence. Outside an old man sat in an aluminum folding chair. The roots of his hair were green and his beard was half yellow. He looked through us like we were flowers or baby rabbits, mysterious and inconsequential.

My father came out of the trailer and we drove down the winding road to the grocery store. We bought hot dogs, buns, and a jar of French's mustard. Dad bought us each a grape Crush and we drank them on the dark drive back. I knew not to ask any questions. Even my brothers, who usually fought for space in the back, were quiet.

My father boiled the hot dogs and we ate at the table under an exposed bulb. After we got into our pajamas, my dad let us go outside into the pagan darkness. Light from inside the trailer was muted on the scaly tree trunks and purple weeds. The crown vetch had tiny thorns and flowers with purple veins. One plant oozed white spittle; another had flies all over the stem.

My father sat on the steps and lit a cigarette, the orange dot moving up and down in the dark as he made a sound like air stuck in a window frame.

In the middle of the night I heard my mother screaming. The door to the bedroom, where my brothers and I slept together, was slanted open so I could see the hallway.

"I won't stay here!" she shrieked. "You can't make me stay in this hellhole."

David sat up and we watched my mother swing her body from side to side as if she were on fire. My father tried to grab her shoulders.

I rolled my eyes at David and he started to laugh. I laughed too, with my hand over my mouth, and we flung ourselves back on the bed and covered our heads with blankets.

A door slammed and my father begged my mother to come out of the bathroom. David hugged his knees in an effort to suppress his laughter. My father rattled the doorknob and pleaded with my mother to come out. After a while my father slid down the wall and sat on the floor.

CHAPTER 8

M Y MOTHER BORROWED MONEY from her parents for
plane tickets and my brothers and I flew north while
my father drove the truck back. That summer we lived with
my father's parents while he worked at a picnic-table factory
and looked for another place to continue his chaplain training. He finally found work at another state hospital. On warm
days patients at Byberry were locked into recreation containers spread out over the expanse of lawn that surrounded the
brick buildings. Gray-faced men and women looked out
through the bars like desultory zoo animals. Stories of the
"crazies," as my mother referred to them, delighted my brothers and me. One man wore a Matchbox car around his neck
and thought he was Speed Racer.

Dad was surprised to find Ralph at Byberry. Ralph explained that over the summer he'd been discharged from Norwich into a halfway house. While living there he realized that
President Nixon needed to be eliminated. So he'd used his SSI
benefits to buy a train ticket to Washington. On the trip he'd
assured his fellow passengers that he was going to assassinate

the president. He was taken off the train at the Philadelphia station by two policemen. The bastards, as Ralph referred to them, had brought him to Byberry. Not that he didn't like the place. The food was better than at Norwich and he confided to my dad that he had a girlfriend. At recreation they had "fun" behind the bushes in back of the power plant.

Every day after school I unlocked the back door of our rented house with the key I kept on a shoelace around my neck. I went to my room and lay out on my bed. I was having trouble making friends, my stutter an impediment to the sort of silly conversations that fifth-grade friendships thrive on, and since I was the new kid the established cliques were wary of me. Besides, I was too worried about my parents' marriage to feel invested in a life of my own. What was a girlfriend or a math test compared to my mother sobbing about how she had wasted *everything*?

The house itself comforted me. The interior was cramped and genteel: hardwood floors, a fireplace, lead glass cabinets in the kitchen, the hum of the radiators, the tiny bubbles in the window glass, the nook off the living room where I practiced my flute. I was discovering the pleasures of solitude. After I finished my homework, I read with a blanket pulled over my knees, devouring books about clever English children. When I couldn't read anymore, I gazed out the window over the grape arbor at the backs of the houses across from ours. Every now and then I'd see an arm or the top of a woman's head awash in fluorescent light. I watched this random movement for hours, as a cat watches fish in an aquarium. I wondered about the lives of the people I saw. Sometimes I made up stories about them. I was beginning to sense how much more complicated life was than I'd originally anticipated, and this observation filled me with a dreamy melancholy. I couldn't communicate how I felt. Every time I tried to speak I couldn't say more than a few words without getting stuck on an initial sound, an *s*, a *ch*, the dreaded *t*. I'd bump on that sound spasmodically until I finally spit out the rest of the letters or substituted a word that was easier to say. When I sang I never stuttered, and some days I'd play Carpenters songs on my cassette player or the Helen Reddy song "I Am Woman," which I'd taped off the radio.

Other days I sat at my desk and wrote in a spiral notebook with a white horse on the cover. Stories mostly, one about a young vampire that went against his bloodsucking family and drank only milkshakes, another based on *The Poseidon Adventure* about a Ferris wheel that spins off to Mars. As I wrote I noticed that some phrases seemed lighter than others. It was a kind of magic how the letters would loosen and float up off the page.

One day after school I found a manila envelope on the welcome mat on our front doorstep. David and Jonathan ran past me into the basement to play while I took the envelope into the living room. I sat on the ottoman and laid it on my lap. There was no address and the envelope had not been sealed; the lip was tucked under. I reached my hand in and pulled out two file folders, one stuck inside the other, both covered with tiny handwritten letters as small as newsprint. On every page a picture was glued into the text. On the first page was the doe-eyed painting of Jesus just like the one that had hung in my grandparents' house. On other pages were pictures cut from the newspaper, one of Michael Jackson and another of Steve Carlton in his Phillies baseball uniform.

The words started at the top edge of the page without addressing anyone in particular. I read the prose with interest. God was angry, angry that Fabian had posed nude in *Playgirl*, angry that Queen Elizabeth had spent the money the cows had given her on the London Bridge. Weather was controlled by the government. Some of the lines were clear; others were unreadable in any traditional way. *Apples to say what no you don't need. Rain door rotten to the money spent.*

The experience of reading something without complete understanding was not unfamiliar to me. I was not the strongest reader and often certain pages in books read, to me, like chaotic passages from insane manifestos. Who could the letter be from? It wasn't like any letter I'd ever seen. The letters I knew were filled with polite, bland language, questions on how school was going and general descriptions of yardwork. This letter, with its prophetic message and odd ritualistic lettering, reminded me of the magic books that appeared mysteriously in fairy circles of trees, or of the stone tablet delivered out of the burning bush. The letter could not have been written, I decided, by a person. It might have been written by a half man, half animal, or by a mythical creature like a giant or a troll. But the language of the letter suggested to me the words I'd heard when my father took me to a black church and an overheated lady had spoken in what my father called tongues. The letter, I decided, must have been written by God.

I could hear the clock ticking on the mantel and felt the late-afternoon sun on my back. I read on with interest, learning that lightbulbs had tiny cameras inside. *For the flower Hanoi, blood from bombs isn't happy.* These tiny cameras watched my father, who shouldn't carry around a Lutheran hymnal. My brothers would have to be punished because of the way he held the book in the crook of his arm. God was angry. God was angry at my brothers David and Jonathan. God was angry that they walked around in their underpants. God was so angry that both my brothers would have to have their penises cut off.

I set the letter on top of the television and went into the

kitchen, picked up the receiver, and dialed the numbers on the index card taped to the wall next to the phone. I stuttered so much it took the department store operator a while to understand my mother's name.

"Lock all the doors," she said after I told her. "Lock all the windows. Go down with your brothers into the basement and wait."

That night a detective in a gray suit came over. He had short red hair and serious, well-organized features. He asked how I'd found the letter and if I'd seen anyone around the front of the house. He wrote notes with his left hand on a legal pad. I answered as best I could, all the time staring at the letter that lay on top of the television. I had not had enough time with it. I wanted to force my hand into a page as if it were a pool of water.

The detective opened his briefcase. Inside were notches for tweezers, scissors, brushes, and little jars of powder. I recognized the detective's briefcase as his version of the traveling communion kit, and I moved down the couch so I could examine it more closely. He put on a pair of thin white gloves, the sort I'd once seen a librarian use to handle an antiquated book, and walked to the television and stood over the letter, his back to us, as he asked questions. Had my brothers ever gone to Byberry? Was there anybody in the neighborhood who acted oddly, hoarded newspapers or glass jars?

My father shook his head as the detective carried the letter in both hands over to his briefcase and slipped it into a plastic bag like the ones used to encase rare comic books.

I was so frightened after the detective left that I did something unthinkable. I invited both my brothers to sleep with me. Before we went to bed we built a block barrier in front of the door. I slipped a loop over the top block and attached a string to the doorknob. If anyone opened the door, the blocks would fall and make a racket. Jonathan didn't understand our predicament but David, just a year younger than me, was clearly afraid. No one had told him what the letter said but he knew by the way my mother had drilled him that it held something ominous.

The hall light was left on and after our mother kissed us, I locked the door. I was conflicted, unsure if we were safer with the door open or closed. It all depended on whether the intruder intended to enter by the door or the window. I knew if the demon had supernatural powers, no material structure could stop him.

Jonathan fell asleep as soon as my mother turned off the overhead light. I heard his breathing stretch and he turned onto his side, drooling gently into the pillow. David was in the middle. We'd decided to sleep oldest to youngest, and though he fought sleep for a while, eventually he turned onto his stomach and his eyelids drifted down.

I lay at the edge of the bed closest to the door listening to traffic rush on the thoroughfare. The radiator clanged and the house stretched, wood against plaster, jostled ever so slightly by the rotating earth. An angle of streetlight fell over the tower of blocks, making it look like the ominous architecture of a deranged civilization.

My heart pounded and my vision was edged with silver minnows like the time I fainted from heatstroke. Often I embroidered the truth and sometimes I sat on David's chest and let spit dangle on my lip over his face. Sin, in my father's sermons, was played down and was answered simultaneously— my father often said, "God forgives immediately"—with redemption. But I was a foxhole pagan, and I had accepted my grandfather's idea of sin and the necessary blood atonement. My sin let evil loose from the supernatural sphere, and now that evil was flying over the tops of houses, through the budding branches, toward my bedroom window.

When he got home the next night my father told us the detective had figured out a patient recently released from the hospital had written the letter, someone my father hardly knew. Though the mystery was solved, he was still preoccupied. On Sunday, when he'd given communion, an elderly man shouted, "Just give me the shit!" He still wore his black suit and white clerical, but his enthusiasm for ministering to crazy people was dissipating. I knew before long we'd be moving again.

CHAPTER 9

WE SPENT OUR FIRST few months in Roanoke, Virginia, in a rented duplex that clung with a dozen others like barnacles on the side of Sugarloaf Mountain. Eventually my parents bought a ranch house in a subdivision off Route 419. Now we had a house and a station wagon. We got a dog, a schnauzer-poodle mix my father named Madel. To my mother's great relief we finally had many of the trappings of normalcy, but we were still uncongealed as a family. My father stayed up late, listening to his jazz records and smoking cigarettes. David kept hamsters in a cage by his bed and was obsessed with nunchuks and BB guns. After school Jonathan changed into his army uniform and spent the afternoons rolling around in the backyard, shooting invisible adversaries. Even Madel was weird, obsessively chasing cars on the road in front of our house and then sleeping on the shoes in my closet.

When my father left in the morning for his job at Mental Health Services, he no longer wore his clerical or carried his communion kit. In sweaters and bell-bottoms he drove to the ramshackle Victorian where he developed programs aimed at helping people communicate. Rather than minister exclusively to mental patients, my dad now developed programs that helped raise the consciousness of people in the community, attacking preconceptions and prejudices. In workshops for hairdressers he explained how they could listen better to their elderly clients, and he created the Aging Game, which he presented at PTA meetings and the Kiwanis club. Once he came to my health class and led my classmates and me in the game, which simulated the frustration of growing older. Players lost motor skills and hearing, got cancer and diabetes, their partners died, and by the end everyone was stuck in a nursing home. A more optimistic project was the one that helped patients recently released from mental hospitals. He'd convinced local churches to provide weekly meals and fellowship.

Once I accompanied my dad to one of these events in a church basement. A dozen dazed people sat in front of paper plates of steaming lasagna while cheerful church ladies in pastel sweater sets made sure everyone had enough lemonade. After we ate, a tall, stately man who owned a local department store brought out a stack of shoe boxes. Each former patient was given a new pair of tennis shoes. After everyone put on their new shoes, the minister's wife rolled out a baked Alaska and used a match to light the meringue. A pink soap-bubble flame encased the cake, and several of the participants jumped up and down in manic ecstasy.

As my father embarked on his quest to foster secular transformation, our family lost track of God. My father said a hurried grace and my mother never mentioned our former proximity to the church. She'd come back to life now that we had a sliver of stability. After setting up house and finding a dentist, a doctor, a new dry cleaner, and a butcher shop, she set about improving my brothers and me. Jonathan, who had learning disabilities, got a tutor. David, who was overweight, was encouraged to exercise. I had my stutter, but my more acute problems were social. I didn't have any friends. This situation wasn't helped by the fact I wore the same plaid pants and acrylic sweater to school every day and that I never washed my hair. My mother took me to the Leggett department store and bought me corduroy skirts and gauze tops. She got me a training bra and insisted that I take a bath every other day. My mother's strategy for transcending her surroundings had been to cultivate her beauty, and while her results were clearly mixed, it was the only method she was familiar with. It was clear I wasn't going to be a beauty, but I could at least keep myself clean.

My mother also gave me advice on how to make friends. If I wanted to be normal I had to try for friends who had already reached a level of perfection. Not the cheerleaders with their shining hair and expert coordination—even my mother knew they were beyond my reach—but the next clique down.

Robin, who led this group, was the most sexually developed girl in the seventh grade. She was tall, big boned, and wore her dirty blonde hair short. Her father, who with his black hair and generous lips looked like an aging Elvis, owned Lakeside Amusement Park. Robin claimed to have menstruated when she was nine and said she'd played both spin the bottle and seven minutes in heaven. Vickie, her childhood friend, was a tomboy. Karen, the group's best-placed member—she was a junior high cheerleader—was the least powerful. Her BO was legendary and she was desperate for a boyfriend.

Robin wasn't hard to make friends with. She always needed an extra girl for her rendezvous with guys at her father's amusement park. I went along as a decoy, wandering in the arcade while Robin made out in the woods behind the roller coaster. More often, though, we'd all spend the night in Robin's basement. The subterranean room had several pinball machines and a dry bar with vinyl stools. We'd spread our sleeping bags out over the shag carpet and gossip about our school's misfits. One girl who had cerebral palsy played the accordion every year in our school talent show, and Robin would mimic her jerking her body from side to side.

Robin put my training bra in the freezer and squeezed Close-Up gel beside my sleeping bag so when I woke in the morning she could tell everyone that I got my period.

One night I kept my bra on and had waited to fall asleep after Robin. I woke to find myself smothered in sleeping bags, the flannel and down heavy on my head. I heard laughter and felt feet pounding and a body slamming against me. I thought I might have been dreaming.

"D-D-D-D-Darcey," Robin said.

"When I call her on the phone," Karen complained, "there is just a silence and I have to say her name. She can't even say hello."

This was true, of course, and I was so ashamed I decided I'd pretend to be asleep. I stayed very still as the girls, one after another, took turns jumping on top of me. I felt Robin's hard breasts, Vickie's calf muscles, Karen's heavily perfumed body odor. After a while Robin's father yelled down the staircase for quiet. In the morning I told Robin's mother I couldn't stay for the chocolate-chip pancakes. On the walk home, through a strip of woods that divided my subdivision from Robin's, I was crying so hard that I had to squat down and balance myself against a tree trunk. At home I lay in my bed, looking at the swirls in the paint pattern. I stayed in bed all day until the streetlights came on and I saw moths flying around in the greenish light. I vowed I would do whatever I could to get rid of my stutter.

The Precision Fluency Shaping Program was connected to Hollins, a women's college not far from my house. My mother, in her continuing effort to help me, had got me a scholarship to the three-week program. On my first day I sat in a lecture hall listening to the founder, Ronald I. Webster, a man in a blue suit with the generous mannerisms of a game show host, talk about the basic ideas intrinsic to his program. No one really knows why people stutter. Most experts agree stuttering has a neurological origin, that it's caused by an organic dysfunction of the brain. It may be genetic. When a stutterer is under stress, serotonin, a neurotransmitter, surges from the right, emotional, side of the brain into the left, logical, side of the brain and blows the complex neurological connection that controls the mechanics of speech.

Webster told us he was convinced the cognitive and emotional components of stuttering resulted directly from the presence of disturbed speech muscle-movement patterns. In this program, he told us, our speech was going to be slowed down and reconstructed. The physical mechanism used in the production of speech was going to be precisely and systematically retrained. We were going to relearn the proper means of producing elemental sounds, rebuilding our ability to produce syllables, words, and ultimately complete sentences.

After the opening meeting, I met with a speech therapist, a young blonde woman named Kitty, and the rest of my therapeutic group: Randy, a quiet teenager in an Aerosmith T-shirt; a priest with an olive complexion and Italian accent; and a Baptist minister of music, a man with frosted hair who played us a cassette of one of his compositions, a song entitled "God's

Not Finished with Me Yet!" Kitty encouraged us to talk about the shame our stutters had caused us.

"To s-s-s-stutter from the p-p-p-pulpit," the priest said, "is most h-h-h-humiliating. I see the ch-ch-ch-children laughing."

"I j-j-just w-w-went right into m-m-m-usic," the minister of music said. "I c-c-c-ouldn't talk so I t-t-t-tried to s-s-s-sing."

"It's h-h-h-ard," I said, "w-w-w-hen I have to r-r-r-ead aloud. I get s-s-stuck on w-w-words."

Kitty's face was sympathetic. "What about you, Randy?"

Randy looked down at his tennis shoes and shrugged.

Stopwatches and workbooks were handed around and Kitty told us from now on each syllable we said had to stretch to two seconds. She demonstrated moving her mouth slowly. *"Frrrooommmmmm noooowwwwwwww ooooooonnnnnnn yoooooouuuurrr sssspeeaaachh wiiiiiiilllllll beeeeee veeeerrrrry slllooooowwwww."*

The speech lab was small, with a white cork ceiling and walls. I sat at a wood table, facing the gentle-onset box. The machine was the size of a toaster oven and completely black except for the green light. In the workbook, columns of *sh*, *ch*, and *st* sounds ran down the pages. I was careful not to constrict my vocal cords and to elongate the sound as Kitty showed us. If I forced air out too hard, the green light shut off and I'd have to start all over. The same sound said so many times made the wood table glow and the green light on the gentle-onset machine liquefy. Every few hours we'd break and, using our stopwatches, we'd have conversations that were so excruciatingly slow and elongated, I felt like a cartoon character.

Near the end of the first week we were allowed to move our

speech up to one second a syllable, and at this speed we were asked to give speeches. The priest, who was becoming the program darling, spoke on Americans' limited knowledge of pasta sauce. In his speech he claimed that fresh pasta tasted better with a little olive oil than with tomato sauce. His fluency was perfect. Randy spoke about the band Led Zeppelin, and the minister of music spoke about electronic keyboards. I was last. I'd written out my speech, which was about the Blue Ridge mountains, on index cards. Right away the bright lecture-hall lights discombobulated me. None of my rhetorical strategies—changing a word midsyllable, bouncing from sound to sound, running words together—was allowed. The first time I hesitated on the word *mountain*, there was a collective sigh from the audience as if I'd missed a free throw at a basketball game, but when I continued to stutter the crowd was silent. Ronald I. Webster sat like a play producer in the last row of the auditorium. I saw him whisper into Kitty's ear, and afterward she took me aside and told me I was never going to reach fluency if I didn't *believe* I could control my stutter.

That weekend I was supposed to take my stopwatch home and time all my conversations. Kitty explained that this was the first step of transference. After years of morbid attention to my speech I'd soon be speaking fluently. No more involuntary caesuras and rapid machine-gun repetition. No longer would I dread the pronunciation of certain words. My family was one thing, but no way was I going to talk to any of my friends in extended speech, so I stayed in my room reading words from the dictionary. I taped myself, then played the tape back and made checks on the words that gave me trouble. I took a break in the midafternoon and fried myself a hamburger. I began to feel uneasy. I was confused. If God made me perfect, as I'd been led to understand, then why did I have to crush out a part of myself? I read the section from the workbook Kitty recommended.

"When entering this program your speech was something that happened to you. Specifically, stuttering happened to you. It should be clear to you by now that you are in control of your speech. In this program you are learning that you must make your own fluency by systematically manipulating your speech."

At the start of the second week I got a new workbook filled with one-, two-, and three-syllable words. I sat in my cork room, my arms pressed into the table edge, my eyes on the green light of the speech monitor. *Trrroooooppp, Trrroooooppp, Trrroooooppp.* The key was to get the air moving up through the mouth before the sound of the first letter started: then, like a rushing river, any sound would be drawn along on the air current. *Trrraaaiiilll, Trrraaaiiilll, Trrraaaiiilll. Crrraaasssh, Crrraaasssh, Crrraaasssh.* The light went off only occasionally and the sounds were a sort of poetry. *Pllleeeaaa, Pllleeeaaa, Pllleeeaaa. Plllooowww, Plllooowww, Plllooowww.*

It was a bit like playing a wind instrument; the continuity of the breath was directly related to the fluidity of the sound. Sounds came through the walls and mixed with my own resonating words. The Catholic priest said his words in slow normal but at a good clip. *Clleeff, Clleeff, Clleeff.* From the other side Randy was more sporadic; I'd hear him sometimes repeat one word, *Roooooof*, for instance, a hundred times followed by a long period of silence.

On breaks the older men sat in the lounge, drank coffee, and, holding their stopwatches, talked about baseball. Randy leaned his long-haired head back on the leather sofa and pretended to sleep. His T-shirt rose up and showed the fine blond hairs on his stomach. At first Kitty had asked him questions about his high school and if he played any sports, but he always just shook his head.

By midweek we'd progressed to two-syllable words. At first the green light on my speech monitor clicked off at the start of every second syllable. It was trickier than the single syllable words; now I had to keep the river of air floating, and rather than launching a single raft, I had to initiate two syllables, a raft with a rope connector. *Cllliii-nnniiic, Cllliii-nnniiic, Cllliii-nnniiic.* After an hour, with some help from Kitty, I got the hang of it. Cupcake. Cuddle. Country. Cotton. Each got the one-syllable treatment. Kitten. Kingdom. Kindness. Sound vibrated in the air, cut free from its meaning. Sometimes after repeating a long column of words I'd feel as if everything—my chair, the desk, the speech monitor, the clinic, reality itself—was peeling back like an orange rind, exposing the pulp of eternity. I was so overwhelmed I'd forget I was practicing. Who was talking? Was that really me? Once I noticed a girl with a pixie haircut in a floral sundress and clunky tire-tread sandals intoning, *Loobbb-ssstteeerr Loobbb-ssstteeerr, Loobbb-ssstteeerr.* By the time I realized it was me, I was back, my eyes fixed on the green light.

The last week of therapy we were allowed to speed our speech up to half a second a syllable, and Kitty gave us each a push-button phone and a list of numbers. The priest got hair salons, the minister of music got restaurants, and Randy got record and music shops. I got ice cream parlors. On a small slip of paper was written my question: What time do you close? In my room I plugged the phone into the jack. The black plastic phone looked formidable in the overhead light as I read the Transferring section of my workbook.

"Part of your job during transfer is to learn how to use correct targets in spite of the effects of emotionality. The telephone is frequently looked upon by stutterers as a source of continuing frustration. A need for immediate, specific verbal response is part of this communication situation. The requirements of immediacy and specificity often seem to lead to disfluent speech. Again, remember you are creating your own instances of fluency or disfluency. Your speech does not just happen to you."

I practiced my line twenty times at two seconds a syllable, twenty times at slow normal, and finally at what Kitty said was the ideal transfer rate of half a second a syllable. I said the line alternately loudly and in a whisper, trying to hit all the targets: full breath, gentle onset, slow change. After I said the line continuously without shutting down the green light of the speech monitor, I decided I was ready. I looked down at the sheet of numbers that had been xeroxed from the phone book and realized, as it was summer, that teenagers would be working in many of the ice cream parlors—including, perhaps, some of my schoolmates. My heart pounded as I punched in the first number and waited while it rang.

Before anyone answered I felt my vocal cords constrict, like two thumbs locked against each other. When a woman said hello, I made a hard onset on the *wh* and my voice went off, *whwhwhwhwh*, like a skipping record. I laid the receiver in its cradle. My hands shook. I was beginning to see how hard my utopian speech skills were going to be to implement. I had a sinking sense that the techniques I was learning might be impossible to use in regular speech. It was like the Lord's Prayer. The words sounded pretty, but what help were they when your mother gave you the silent treatment?

Maybe I should rephrase my line? *Could you please tell me*

what time you close? But the *c* was just as hard as the *wh*, and the *t* coming off *please* would be hellish. *Please tell me when you close?* That was a possibility, but there was no telling if I could get the river of air steady enough to initiate the *pl* sound, and besides, the phrase sounded rude. I decided to stick with the original, which I said at slow normal fifty times while I tried to regulate my breathing over my frantic heartbeat.

It was impossible. I was too worked up over the line. The line was doomed, each word a gravestone. I decided I'd have to try something drastic: to change the line completely. My experience in managing my stutter had shown me that sometimes a major renovation of a sentence was the only solution. I dialed the Baskin-Robbins in Tanglewood Mall.

"Hello!" a male voice said.

"When do you open?" I blurted.

"Why, we're open right now," he said. "So come on down and get your ice cream!"

I laughed. "Why, thanks!" I said, and hung up.

Three more calls were equally successful. I had slight hesitations but nothing major. Look at me, I thought, I'm talking on the telephone. I should call up President Carter and have a little chat.

The next number was for a place called Rowley's Gas and Ice Cream. Probably just a refrigerator case filled with ice cream sandwiches and Fudgsicles.

"Ha-low," a lady said.

"Whhaatt tiiimmme dooo yooouu opppeeen?" I said.

There was a pause in which I heard through the receiver a country song playing on the radio and the sound of a screen door hitting a wood frame.

"Don't you mean, 'What time do you close?'"

I didn't say anything.

"I don't know who you people are," she said. "I have no idea if you are trying to get my goat pretending to be zombies or robots or whatever. But please stop calling here—you and your people have been calling here every couple weeks for years. We're open at eight and we close at eight. Just stop fucking calling."

She slammed down the phone and I placed the receiver gently in its cradle.

CHAPTER 10

R EVEREND STRAUS WAS A heavy man with a soft body
and a rectangular head. His face was always red, and he
sweated in all kinds of weather and in every situation. His
brow was shiny and the hair around his face damp and darkened with perspiration. He tugged continually at his white
plastic clerical as if he were choking, and yanked his pants up
over his doughy waist. During services at Good Shepherd
Lutheran in Roanoke, Reverend Straus often lost his place
while preaching and looked up at the congregation through
his thick glasses, blinking and bewildered. During communion he'd drop the wafers and get down on his knees to gather
them up. He splashed wine from the common cup onto the
lace collars of the ladies.

Worst was confirmation class, which David and I had to
attend every Wednesday night. We met in the cement-block
church basement under fluorescent light, a half dozen
teenagers slumped in metal folding chairs. Darci Wunkling
was the only one my age, a tall girl with long, dangling arms
and an oblong face covered with acne. Her ashy hair hung in

greasy clumps around her face and she wore JCPenney jeans and rugby shirts. My father encouraged me to be friendly to Darci. Not that he was hanging out with any of the male church members. We joined the church so he could maintain his affiliation, which he needed to keep his job, but I could tell he felt superior to the men, who were mostly insurance salesman or in middle management. Begrudgingly I sat beside Darci in confirmation class, trying to make it clear by my body language that while I would sit by her at church events, this would not be possible in school. Darci was a quiet, unassuming sort of girl with large hands and gentle, brown eyes; she seemed pleased by my proximity.

Sometimes we studied the Bible; other Wednesdays, the Apostles' Creed or the Lord's Prayer. Reverend Straus regularly tripped over the metal Sunday school chairs and lost hold of his notes, the typed pages sailing around the room. He explained, his face pink and covered with sweat, that, unlike pagans who thought the soul was immortal no matter how people behaved during their time on earth, Lutherans believed that the soul's bid for immortality relied solely on a person's relationship to Jesus Christ. He told us that Lutherans believed that death is the penalty for sin. He told us all this like a discombobulated yet compassionate prison guard, passing on the warden's instructions.

When he asked for questions I was flummoxed. What he was saying was as far away from my childhood understanding of the living God as a cement block was from a waterfall. The doctrine reminded me of the rules I was studying in driver's education about not parking near a fire hydrant and how to signal when you pulled into the passing lane.

My classmates and I were all taken with the idea that the early Christians had been persecuted. Busted by the authorities when caught performing a small surreal activity, Christians would draw a fish in the sand to recognize one another. I would often think of two Christians with beards and intense eyes in cream-colored robes, one moving a stick in the sand to form a fish's outline. Since therapy, my speech still wasn't perfect. I stuttered occasionally, but my improved fluency made me want to do things I had never done before. I was anxious to play the lawyer pacing back and forth in front of Darci, who played the doomed Christian sitting in a lone chair. The rest of my classmates were judge and jury.

"Is it true you b-believe the wafer is the body of Christ?" I asked incredulously.

Darci always shook her head, her dirty hair swaying.

"Yes."

"Is it indeed true you believe the weakest s-slave is as good as a rich man?"

"Yes."

"I assume you also believe that the criminal J-Jesus is the son of God."

"Yes," Darci whispered.

"I can't hear you," I said.

"Yes. Yes. I do," she said loudly.

"Judge and j-jury, I ask you to condemn this woman for her foolish beliefs. She is clearly a Christian."

The jury only needed a minute to jot down a verdict and pass the slip of paper to the judge, who read out "Guilty," and then the punishment: either stoning, death in the fiery furnace, or, the class's favorite, death in the Colosseum by the jaws of a lion. Darci slumped forward, her spine pressing out of her striped rugby shirt, as the jury chanted, "Death! Death! Death! Death!" Reverend Straus sat there blinking, yanking at his collar, sweat making the material under his arms inky black, as our parents' cars began to pull off the highway and gather in the dark parking lot.

After years of focusing on me, my mother's improvement plan finally turned to herself; she was taking classes at the community college. At night she'd lay her cardboard piano over the dining room table and move her hands silently around on the keys. She read fat textbooks and worked on her papers about Aztecs and how Picasso developed Cubism. My father, when he was home, which wasn't often, would get into bed, pull the covers to his chin, and read Judith Krantz novels, pausing occasionally to sip tea out of a Snoopy coffee cup. That year he'd lost thirty pounds on the Death Valley Diet. He ate nothing for breakfast, an apple for lunch, and a stew of celery, potatoes, and carrots for dinner every night.

My parents each seemed to have forgotten that the other existed. Nearly every year I had to call my father at work to remind him of my mother's birthday, and my mother's silent treatments seemed perpetual. Once, while she was browning hamburger at the stove, my father came into the kitchen and asked about his dry cleaning. My mother just continued moving the meat around in the fry pan until my father left, his legs moving slowly as if he were pulling them through muddy water. Anger had gone under and now there was exhaustion, an exhaustion that infiltrated the whole house. The living room was empty except for a ficus plant and a beanbag chair, the carpet stained with our dog's training accidents, blotches of gray on the gold shag. The shower in my parents' bedroom was so covered in mold my brothers called it the Devil's Lair.

I was inhibited, but I found ways to rebel. *Mein Kampf* was three times as thick as the young-adult novels surrounding it, and the cover was black with gothic lettering. I didn't know much about Hitler except that he'd had that funny mustache and was at the far end of the pool when it came to absolute evil. I carried *Mein Kampf* sheepishly to the library circulation desk and brought it home in my backpack.

That evening I locked my bedroom door and, lying on my Holly Hobbie bedspread surrounded by stuffed animals, I tried to read the turgid prose. I knew Hitler had killed Anne Frank and that a man responsible for the death of such a beautiful soul was demonic. I knew this, but I also liked the illicit feeling reading the book gave me. It wasn't the holy feeling, but it was a counterweight to the bleakness of my life. I was a blonde-haired teenager living in a brick ranch house attending a church lined with felt banners that said JOY! RE-JOICE! PEACE! But I was also a weepy creature ruled by base longings and haunted by rage and melancholy.

Sex was the most obvious outlet. At my high school the other minister's daughter, Susan Hill, had already bleached her hair blonde and wore blue eye shadow and crusty mascara. Her father's Baptist church was adjacent to our backyard and I'd heard that Reverend Hill got his suit jacket wet all the way to the shoulders when he baptized members in the tank of water that sat to the side of the altar. Every Friday night during the fall you could find Susan in the ditch under the bleachers making out, and between classes she would French kiss her boyfriend of the week in front of her locker. Once, from our back bathroom window, I saw her crawl out from under her father's church bus without her shirt on, her substantial breasts exposed to the parking lot light.

I was too shy to join the Black Sabbath kids who on weekends practiced satanic rituals in each other's rec rooms. All I could manage was to carry *Mein Kampf* around in my book bag. After a while I began to pull the book out at home while I was watching television. My mother frowned and my father called me crazy, but both seemed too tired to argue. At school Robin and my other friends were only interested in talking about the cute boys in *Tiger Beat*. Only my social studies teacher, a tall woman with a long, earnest face, asked why I was carrying around Hitler's life story.

"I want to understand the mind of an evil genius."

"And why is that?" she said, her brow furrowed.

"I'm thinking of becoming one," I said.

Her eyes opened wide. Wanting to emulate Hitler must have been a new low.

"Do your parents know you're reading that book?"

"Yes," I said. "They don't care."

"If you were my daughter," she said, collecting textbooks off each desk, "I would be very upset."

The next Sunday Reverend Straus was sick and my father agreed to fill in for him. As he began to preach, I pulled *Mein Kampf* out of my backpack, balanced it on the pew in front of me, and pretended to read. I stared down at the pages and thought about the cowboy boots I was paying off on layaway at the Leather House at Tanglewood Mall. My father's face registered no surprise during his sermon or while he was giving communion. Even during the benediction, "Go in peace, serve the Lord," he appeared composed.

After the coffee hour, my father sent my mother and brothers home and asked that I stay behind to help him clean up the sacristy. The circles under his eyes sagged and his hands shook as he put the extra wafers away in a Christmas cookie tin, then used a sponge to wipe up spots of wine from the countertop. For a while I thought he was going to give me a lecture, but then I realized I was here to watch him clean; he had the demeanor of a deposed king forced now to do janitorial work. He washed out the silver communion cup and began to rub it dry with a piece of felt.

"That book is impossible to read," I blurted out when I couldn't stand it any longer.

He set the shining chalice beside the bottle of emerald dish soap. "I bet it is," he finally said.

During one Wednesday confirmation class Reverend Straus got the movie projector out and we watched the old film *Martin Luther* projected against the concrete wall. Niall MacGinnis wore a brown robe and a goofy bowl hairdo. His freak-out during the thunderstorm was a mass of frantic close-ups, eyes bulging, eyebrows raised, as his hand clenched a quill pen and he wrote out the Ninety-five Theses.

When the lights came on Reverend Straus began to tell us with great passion about Martin Luther. He'd been uncomfortable about church doctrine, but Reverend Straus clearly had no ambivalence about Luther. Luther, he told us, was the only one who realized that the selling of indulgences was corrupt and that God could exist outside of ornate papal ceremonies. As he spoke, his face was still pink and sweaty, but I realized these were not simply signs, as I'd first thought, of his nerdiness. Reverend Straus showed, in his complete engagement, a spark of divinity.

"Here I stand. I can do no other. God help me. Amen," Straus said, as he repeated Luther's famous line, one I would soon use when refusing to load the dishwasher or to give the dog a bath.

In an effort to get us away from the mock trial, Straus

closed each class by showing us a practical component of Lutheranism. One week we'd visited the sacristy, a novelty for my classmates, and were allowed to hold the communion cup. This particular day he was going to put on his robes, which he had laid over a Sunday school table. First he buttoned up the black alb, then he pulled the white surplice with the square neck over his head. By the time he draped the purple stole around his neck, he was sweating so profusely that drops of water fell onto the crosses embroidered in gold thread on each end. Sitting as we were at the end of the basement closest to the highway, an accelerating truck occasionally drowned out Straus's meandering explication of his ceremonial garb.

After he placed the silver pectoral cross over his head, he leaned forward, balancing a hand on the movie projector beside him. There was a rush of material as his glasses flew off and he and the projector fell onto the linoleum with a resounding crash. He lay there covered with splintered pieces of black plastic, blinking up at the ceiling, while my classmates and I tried not to laugh.

While not as spastic as Reverend Straus, at fifteen I was also gangly and awkward, slow to make the transition from childhood to adolescence. One Easter during communion, as I watched ladies in pastel dresses file up the middle aisle, a thickness grew in my abdomen until it became unbearable. I rushed down to the church bathroom and locked myself in a stall. I lifted my skirt and knew right away from the patch of darkness seeping up from the crotch of my pantyhose that something was wrong. When I pulled them down I saw a bright splotch of red soaked into the white cotton fabric. The curse, as Robin called it, had come. Finally! Hallelujah! I shoved toilet paper into my panties and listened to the organist bang out "Jesus Christ Has Risen Today," my favorite of the hymns we sang on Easter.

At first I thought it was all in my mind how the man at the pizza place, sitting with his kids, watched me walk to the bathroom, or how the cashier at the record store stared as I flipped through the bin of eight-tracks. My stutter was mostly manageable, I'd grown my blonde hair out long, and I'd begun to take an interest in what I wore. I was no longer a misfit. I now had equal footing with my high school friends. At school and while I was walking in the mall, teenage boys and men stared at me. For the first months I assumed I had toothpaste on my shirt or gum stuck in my hair, but as time went on I realized something had changed. I was no longer skinny and ghostlike. I had somehow become appealing. After feeling invisible for so long, I began to crave attention. I wanted that attention to multiply and solidify. My mother had modeled in high school, so when a guy in my neighborhood asked if he could take my picture, my mother agreed even though he was a little creepy, with his brush cut and lair-like basement.

While he had assured me his parents would be home, the only sign of them as I walked through his house was his mother's decorative plate collection and his father's pile of automobile magazines. Better than the outfit I brought with me, black velvet pants and a frilly white blouse, he liked the pink terry-cloth short set I had on and he asked me to stand up against a maple in his yard. He took a few shots of my profile before asking me to turn my back to him.

The photograph he gave me was terrible. I'd broken my nose in a pillow fight at a slumber party, and the bump on my bridge was prominent. My face looked swollen and my chin stiff, as though I was grinding my teeth. Still, to me the black-and-white picture represented my value. From reading *Mademoiselle*, I knew that models had "books" they took around to "go sees." The black binder I bought at Kmart was cheap looking, but I was still proud as I slid the photograph into the clear plastic sleeve. A friend of my father's, a hippie weaver, asked me to model one of her ponchos for the local newspaper. Through the weaver's ad I got a call from Roanoke's only fashion photographer.

Seth Chatwin was a short man with acne scars. He had the account for the local women's clothing store, and businesses came to him if they wanted ads for their restaurant or condominium complex. Once I had seen him shooting pictures of a heavily made-up girl in a tube top and miniskirt in front of the Ground Round on the highway. In our small town, he was the pinnacle of glamour, and when he called me the voice on the other end of the line might as well have been Eileen Ford's. He told me to bring a selection of outfits and to come to his studio, which was in a strip mall adjacent to Terrace Mall.

My mother was enthusiastic about my new modeling opportunities. She helped me pick outfits for the photo shoots and encouraged me to use a cream conditioner on my split ends. Before she'd become Miss Albany, she'd been her town's fashion it girl, posing for photographs, appearing in department store fashion shows, even hosting a Saturday fashion radio program. My father acted indifferent, his relationship to beauty complicated by religion. I knew outward beauty was important to my dad—two of his brothers had also married beauty queens—but he always felt obliged to insist on the primacy of inner beauty, rather than the more vulgar material kind.

The next day after school my mother drove me to the studio. Seth Chatwin wore a leather vest over a polyester blouse with puffy, poetic sleeves. His hair brushed the edge of his thick collar and a few black chest hairs, like insect antenna, curled out from the V of his shirt. Seth disapproved of my outfits—"Don't you have anything that pops?"—though he finally settled on a frilly burgundy shirt and a pair of designer jeans. I changed in the tiny bathroom with a filmy toilet and filthy mop while he moved around outside, adjusting the halogen lights and throwing a Rolling Stones eight-track into his stereo. "Brown Sugar" came on so loud the hollow bathroom door vibrated. When I came out the overhead light was off and all I could see was a dozen black umbrellas and what looked like a movie screen.

"We're trying to get your essence," Seth said as he adjusted one of the umbrellas, which was silver on the inside. "The you in you."

I stepped into the pocket of light. The symbolism wasn't lost on me. I was, for the hour I stood in that spot like a reliquary, a saint statue set up among votive candles. The black circle of Seth's zoom lens butted out through the light and glinted like a fish scale. He told me to move to the music. To be free. To relax. He told me to put my hand in my hair, to jut my chest out. To relax. He told me to angle my hips and to tip up my chin. I gave the camera my best seductive look, an expression I'd developed from studying the faces of women in porno magazines.

The night before I was confirmed, I prepared for the ceremony the way I did for a photo shoot. By now I'd appeared in an ad for Stonehenge apartments and for Chubbies, a new bar out by the airport. I set up my beauty altar and began my elaborate beauty routine. I mixed and then spread a concoction of egg and mayonnaise over my hair, wrapped Saran Wrap around my head, and lay down on my bedspread with two round cucumber slices resting on my eyes. I was enthralled with the advice in my *Seventeen* magazine about soaking your elbows in grapefruit halves and making sure, when your legs were together, that three inches remained between your thighs. From Robin I'd borrowed a long white gauze dress and I was going to wear my Candies with the plastic high heels.

On Sunday morning I rose at six a.m. to shower and blow-dry my hair. Hot curlers were next, followed by the curling iron touch-up. I went through a can of hair spray a week to maintain a style that, at its best, was at least four inches high. At church I sat in the front pew next to Darci Wunkling, who looked like a male nurse in white pants, a white blouse, and a white pair of earth shoes. Darci had recently walked up to me at school while I was with Robin and my girlfriends. I'd said I had to get to class and pulled my group away from her. Darci stood there, uncertain, her long, gangly arms by her sides and sadness falling over her features like a veil.

Reverend Straus called us each by name and I pulled up my long dress and walked like Genevieve to the altar to stand with my classmates.

"These young people," Reverend Straus said, pushing up his glasses and tugging at his clerical, "have each written a statement of what God has done for them."

I still have the bulletin insert. One boy wrote a poem that began: "The creator who made the earth in six days/Sure does work in mysterious ways." Most of the testimonials focused on gratitude for family. Darci wrote: "God gave me a mother and a father and two brothers. God gave me a good home and safety and did not let me get any kind of disease." My own began: "While thinking about writing this paper, I thought, really what has HE given me?" I concluded that God had given me everything. It seems a little canned and while I don't remember my father helping, I suspect the high rhetoric of the last line—"And when I am confirmed, Christ will have given me one more thing, the gift of his body and blood"— came from him.

After we each read our testimonial, Reverend Straus asked us to kneel at the altar rail. I was a nubile virgin waiting for the wizard's blessing, but Reverend Straus was more like the court jester as he dropped his Lutheran book of worship, the gold-edged pages fluttering, and wiped his brow with what looked like a paper towel tucked into his sleeve. He placed his hand on one head after another. *May God bless and keep you in this Christian life.* When he came to David and me, he hesitated, and I felt my heart bang against my rib cage. He was going to announce that I was more concerned with which shampoo made my hair smell best than the tenets of the Nicene Creed. He would tell about my growing fascination with prostitution and how nearly every day I mocked the sacraments by kneeling on the tiles in the bathroom and kissing the corner of the terry-cloth towel.

I heard the doors open at the back of the church and saw my father strolling up the center aisle in his robes and pectoral cross, the one he made himself out of clay and beach glass. He jumped onto the altar like a rock star. His blond sideburns were long and his face tan from gardening. At first I worried he had decided that Reverend Straus was too incompetent to confirm us, that there would be a power struggle, two men in white and black robes, each trying to get his palm onto the top of our heads. But when I glanced up I saw that Reverend Straus had a look of parental indulgence over his features. He and my father must have planned this last-minute intercession. I was a little annoyed that my dad was upstaging us by making a surprise appearance as our confirmer. Besides, though I'd never tell anybody, I had been looking forward to Reverend Straus confirming me. He may have been a fool, but even I had to concede he was a holy one.

Dad laid his hand on my brother's head. I kept my eyes on the communion rail. When he laid his hand on my head, I felt the warmth of his palm moving into my hair follicles. He insisted on being our conduit to God. When I glanced up, his face was not the theatrical mask I'd anticipated. His features were drawn, almost skeletal. I saw the beach-glass chalice embedded in his clay cross and how his Adam's apple quivered as he looked up into the track lighting. I wasn't really sure if my father believed in God anymore. Outside of church I'd never seen him pray, and he mostly read popular novels—*The Thorn Birds* and *Looking for Mr. Goodbar*—but his voice quivered as he blessed me, and I knew that his faith hadn't gone completely, that he still clung to a particle of belief.

CHAPTER 11

I WAS COMMITTED NOW to glamour. Seth Chatwin called me every few months and I relished the time I spent in his strip-mall studio under the hot lights. I had begun to date both *Dukes of Hazzard* middle linebackers with their Jeeps and chewing tobacco and lawyers' sons who attended the ritzy local private school and drank Maker's Mark out of monogrammed flasks. My upper-middle-class dates treated me to expensive dinners and then took me down to their finished basements, where we sat on velvet love seats restored by their polite and chilly mothers and they'd play their Who and Genesis records. I liked the prints of British fox hunts and the magnolia wallpaper. The boys from Bent Mountain rode me up the mud hill after a keg party to catch the end of the dirty movie at the 220, the porno drive-in. What all the boys had in common was they were less interested in talking than making out.

Our next-door neighbors, the Sladers, fascinated me. Their house smelled of musk oil and contained an entertainment center with hundreds of eight-track tapes and a waterbed with a spread made of fake fur. Charlie Slader was balding, cheerful, and good-looking. He managed the local beverage-distribution center in Roanoke. Diana, his wife, was about ten years younger. She worked as a secretary at one of the local advertising agencies and was the most glamorous woman in the neighborhood. She had one of those high-cheekboned, stretched-skin faces that looked good at every angle, and her blunt-cut blonde hair had both aristocratic and sexual connotations. Her charisma was in no way diminished by the fact that she'd had a previous family. She'd been married to a bartender in Texas and had a son named Daniel. The boy lived with his father and came to visit Diana two weeks a year in August. I babysat him the summer before, a sweet, hyper kid who continuously begged me to let him call his father and stepmother in Fort Worth. Three minutes would pass and he'd ask me again: "Please let me call my dad!"

Diana Slader became my role model. Unlike my mother, who had blown her chance at love and happiness, Diana had parlayed her looks into something tangible. She was proof that my beauty rituals would eventually pay off. Since I'd babysat for her son, she'd taken to giving me makeup: expensive stuff from the last good department store downtown. She gave me clothes too—a silk blouse with a tiny snag, or pants she no longer liked the cut of. Once, she sat me down and explained with extreme seriousness the magic properties of vitamin E oil, how the thick, sticky stuff had completely erased the stretch marks left by her pregnancy.

When Charlie Slader appeared in a Coke commercial filmed nearby, the couple's glamour barometer hit its high point. With residual checks they bought a Jacuzzi, a black leather sectional sofa, and a Corvette. The Sladers once showed up at the pizza parlor where I waitressed to see J. P., the former minor league sports star who owned the place. I called over to the little white house next door where J. P. and his partner ran a successful side business in cocaine. He told me to send the Sladers right over.

A week before Thanksgiving, Diana called and invited me to be an extra in a commercial for a local furniture store her agency was filming that night. I'd been in print ads, but television was something different, its small screen as powerful as an aleph in our bland suburban lives. I began my beauty rituals immediately. My mother handed me each hot roller, her face radiant. Glamour was her religion and, though its elusive precepts had let her down again and again, she clung to its promise.

At the modern house in the new-money subdivision where the commercial was to be filmed, ten well-dressed couples milled around drinking spiked eggnog and eating Christmas cookies. On the way to the bathroom, I walked past a bedroom where Diana was practicing. She held a sprig of mistletoe and, with bright eager eyes, repeated her single line over and over. A man with a pot belly and thick black eyebrows, whom I guessed was the advertising agency's director, encouraged her to relax, to put her shoulders down and lower her voice. "Oh, I know," she said, regressing into her East Texas twang. "I'm so stiff." While she looked beautiful, there was something desperate in the awkward way she held her mouth.

When I returned to the living room, the cameraman was adjusting his television lights. Under the hot bulbs I saw a woman's long orange fingernails and another's beige foundation lines. The TV extras were getting a little drunk. A man told a dirty joke about Santa Claus. A woman snorted at the punch line and a younger woman dropped her cup of eggnog. All the glamour had drained out of the moment. In a few days at the Christmas eve service I'd hold a candle and sing "Silent Night." My doll Kimmie no longer played baby Jesus, but the flame would illuminate another baby doll wrapped in a blanket. I was conflicted. I wanted to be good and to be beautiful. I decided I'd tone down my beauty routine; from now on I'd only use the big hot curlers, I'd limit myself to blue eye shadow—no more greens or purples—and I'd wear only clear nail polish, no more red.

In the spring, Charlie Slader came to our door to invite my parents over. He stood in our kitchen wearing his sport shirt with the Budweiser logo. With the money from the commercial he'd gotten his teeth capped and kept himself perpetually tan. Both his bald spot and his gold horseshoe ring shone in the overhead light as he explained to my parents, in his North Carolina drawl, that he had a business venture to discuss with them.

My mother was pleased and even my father, who was usually immune to the world's diversions, seemed flattered. They got dressed up. My mother wore an orange pantsuit with puffy sleeves and advised Dad not to wear his black clerical, to go instead as a layman, in khakis and a blue sport coat. They'd been in love once and in that moment, as I watched them walk down the grassy hill to the Sladers', I could only hope that their luck might change, that they'd figure a way out of their calcified indifference.

Hours later they returned. My mother's face was relaxed, my father's beaming. They talked conspiratorially in the kitchen, sharing a cup of instant coffee and kissing. The business proposition concerned something called Amway, a company that sold "extraordinary" soap products. My mother got dressed the next morning and sat at the kitchen table reading over the Amway materials. In the evening, she and my dad compiled lists of friends and family who would buy the miraculous soap. When, a few days later, the sample arrived through the mail—an unassuming cardboard box—I stared at it for a long time before opening the lid and gazing at the mundane-looking soap crystals. I felt confused. Mrs. Efrain, the Avon lady in our neighborhood, sold makeup door to door but her kids still wore acrylic sweaters. I wanted to believe that the enchantment fallen over my parents was viable. So I begged them to take me to the group meeting that night at the Slader home.

Plates of cheese biscuits and candied pecans lay on the Sladers' glass coffee table. Their black leather sofa glittered under the chrome ball lights. I sat on the carpet listening to Charlie tell how Amway had transformed his life, giving him financial security, self-esteem, and those special items—a nice car, exotic vacations, pretty things for the wife—most people were uncomfortable admitting made life worthwhile. He paused at this point and asked Diana to show us her newest acquisition. She walked out into the hallway and returned wearing a long silver fox, the collar turned up movie star style, strains of white fur highlighting her cheekbones and cornflower eyes. Everyone was mesmerized. Charlie suggested that Diana let some of the ladies try on her coat. And my mother, as if under a spell, rose from where she sat on the couch and let Diana arrange it over her shoulders. In the coat, with her body hidden, my mother appeared much younger, more like the girl who twenty years earlier had worn a beauty queen's coat and married a minister to get away from her drunken father. Her features froze in an expression of dangerous pleasure, an expression mirrored in my father's face.

The moment didn't last. Within a month my mother was back in her bathrobe, my father hardly ever home. My mother moved around the house doing laundry, loading the dishwasher. She was miserable, tormented. It was my last summer at home, and the temperature in our house sometimes crept to 100. I watched her lumber down the hallway carrying a plastic laundry basket filled with towels, her face gray and contorted with frustration.

Every day after work my father sat at the dining room table working on what he called his masterpiece. Spread out around him were reels of movies in blue canisters: Thanksgivings, Christmases, family vacations, all recorded on black strips of celluloid. At Kmart Dad had bought a splicing machine as well as a few cheap movies. He worked on his masterpiece every night until bedtime.

After a month he called us together after dinner for the premiere. We sat in the living room, my mother on the beanbag chair and my brothers and me beside her on the floor. My dad switched off the lights and flipped on the projector. Light shot out of the lens, illuminating dust particles in the air. My brothers and I were walking along the beach, our hair catching the pink sunset. Jonathan, then four, squatted down to look at a ghost crab in the bubbly surf. Jump-cut to a monster with a long snout stomping a fishing village; now back to the beach where David held up a starfish; then the monster's eyes were filled with a vague reptilian sadness as he threw his head back and howled at the moon. David and I held pastel Italian ices out in front of the duplex in Norwich; the monster showed his terrible teeth; I sat on a rocking chair at a motel on our way to Kentucky; the monster's webbed feet crushed an automobile. Footage lurched back and forth in time. I saw that my father was more interested in the transitions than in the time sequence. As the movie progressed, the cuts got faster and my father, as projectionist, used his hand to keep his splicing from slipping. He wore madras shorts and one of his short-sleeved black clericals open to show a T-shirt. His bare legs were crossed and he laughed at some of the quick juxtapositions: people fleeing an apartment building; David and me, in new clothes, getting on the school bus. As the film went on, he laughed more loudly, head thrown back. For a while my brothers laughed along with him until the sequences grew incoherent, cuts so quick they resembled subliminal flashes.

My mother's body in the beanbag was covered with shifting movie light and her whole face was wet as if tears leaked right through her skin. The monster crushed a helicopter in his long-fingernailed paw; I walked down the steps of the rectory in Southington, waving, wearing my strawberry-print sundress; David followed carrying a half-eaten apple; and then Jonathan, who had just learned to walk, held on to the railing with both hands and stretched his little legs down step to step. We stood in front of the rectory, three towheaded children blinking in the bright sun before the camera swung sideways to show a long shot of the church.

PART THREE

CHAPTER 12

I MET COLIN IN COLLEGE, during my junior year abroad. Compared to the beefy boys I dated in America, he was a different species altogether. He wore a blue suit tailored perfectly to the contours of his delicate frame. He was, as he took the podium, relaxed and confident. The debate was on homosexuality. His premise was that people were drawn to one another's souls rather than their genitalia. Sexuality could not be bracketed and slotted under a particular heading.

A few days later I sat in a pub listening to him and drinking one gin and tonic after another while he drank and chain-smoked Silk Cuts. Compared to Colin I spoke like a cave woman. Listening to him talk was like watching open-heart surgery, a high-wire acrobat, and a thunderstorm all at the same time. I could tell by the way he was showing off that he was interested in me, but that interest was muted and ambivalent.

After a few drinks he spoke of the choirmaster at his Catholic elementary school and the loneliness of the man's life, particularly his solitary dinners of rashers and eggs. His eyes bulged slightly, the blue irises bright through the haze of smoke. He was quiet as he blew out a long feathery tendril.

"Why," he finally said, "do people have to live with such sorrow?"

On the way home down the narrow stone streets of Cork city, I followed him into a dark church and, the tails of his raincoat flying out behind him, he fell to his knees in front of a statue of the Virgin Mary.

Desire had become my life's organizing principle. The intensity of my desire was more important than if the object that initiated the desire was worthwhile. In fact, I found that my desire was stronger and purer in form if the object, in this case Colin, was aloof and nihilistic. Fucking Colin was like fucking a current of warm water; in bed he pressed against me gently, his scent a mixture of gin and smoke. We'd kiss for a while and then he'd roll to the bed's edge and look up at the ceiling. His inattention had a holy quality.

Sexuality wasn't something I'd been able to talk to my parents about. My mother suggested sex was unpleasant—the sperm runs down your leg—and insisted I wait till marriage. She'd gone ballistic when, helping me move into my dorm freshman year, she'd found contraceptive sponges. My father was silent on the subject, though before I went away to school he took me out to lunch. We were nearly done with dessert when he told me I could come to him him even if the p-word happened. Because of the blank at the center of my parents' intimate life, my own desire played out in a vacuum.

I drank a lot, though my craving for drink was nothing compared to my sexual appetite. I was in an agitated state, a hot, coiled feeling between my legs, chain-smoking cigarettes as I walked with Colin to his apartment, a subterranean room with twin beds, a huge wood wardrobe between them, and heavily curtained windows. Sometimes we fucked in the afternoon in my room in the house I shared with other American students. Afterward we ate cream-cheese-and-pineapple sandwiches and drank Blue Nun wine.

Several times a week I'd look down at a dozen empty gin and tonic glasses and then at Colin, who was talking about Harold Pinter, the *New York Review of Books*, or, if he was really drunk, the lonely choirmaster. Once he jumped up onto the bar and claimed to be exhuming President Kennedy's body for the debating team's upcoming party. His older brother, Gerard, asked us if we were children of the calm or children of the storm. More than once, after an afternoon of drinking, as we walked in the rain toward Colin's place, we ran into the local bishop and Colin knelt down to the hem of his robe and kissed his ring. After he'd admitted he'd slept with a friend of mine, I felt, while we fornicated drunkenly, that I would ignite like tissue paper I'd seen a boy put a match to. I felt as if I'd rise up hot and weightless before disappearing completely.

In May, as the school year ended, I realized I couldn't go back to America. If I went back to the States, I wasn't sure who I'd be. I told my parents I wasn't coming home and immediately they stopped sending my weekly allowance. Three years earlier when I'd left home for college, I'd felt liberated to be away from my mother's misery and my father's indifference. In my mind America had taken on the qualities of my parents' unhappiness. There was no way I was going back. I was down to my last five quid when I heard I'd won my college's literary contest in absentia. Colin and I moved to Dublin with the five-hundred-dollar prize money.

* * *

We lived in a one-room flat with Colin's childhood friend Adrian, who was studying Gaelic at the university. Adrian wore his hair in a monk's bowl cut and always looked melancholy. All Adrian's friends were scholars. Colson Dean was a young classics major with a lovely head of curly hair, one lock falling with cinematic precision over his pale brow. Patsy Logan was an Auden scholar. And David O'Donnel, a porcine man studying Nabokov, answered every question with a line from *Pale Fire*. He wore an ascot and a monocle and was known as the Diva. Once, when Colin and I stayed at his apartment, I heard him say into the bathroom mirror, "And how does the Diva look this morning?" His own voice answered: "Disgusting as usual!" Nearly every afternoon we met in the Bailey, a bar near Trinity College.

Within a month my prize money was gone and Colin borrowed money first from friends and then from radio station coworkers. He worked sporadically at RTE, playing a farmer or a priest in radio plays. His pay was minimal, thirty or forty quid that disappeared in an evening of drinking. I was, according to Colin, to get a job as an art gallery girl, to wear a sleeveless black linen dress with pearls and leather pumps. The only problem, besides that I did not have working papers, was that Dublin had only a few galleries, all of them staffed by men in two-button blazers who were incredulous that I'd be so delusional as to think I had the credentials to work around art.

After he had several drinks, Colin flirted with both men and women. One night he got so drunk Adrian and Patsy volunteered to help me get him home. When I tried to remove his tenth gin and tonic, he held the glass above my head, his lips slipped back to show his teeth, and he growled.

In the morning, after Adrian went off to the library, Colin sat in his bathrobe at the small table by the front window with his tea, looking miserable and contrite. I pretended to write in my journal, all the while staring at him, willing him, as I used to will my cup of milk to move, to think about *me*. After a while Colin put on his single of Sid Vicious singing "My Way" and smoked, the sound of the fire burning through the tiny shards of tobacco was exquisite in the silence between songs.

Around the corner from the flat was a gray stone church with big red double doors. I heard the bell and I decided to go. The bald rector gave a sermon on Jesus's laserlike healing power. With my stomach growling—several days had passed without food—I recited prayers along with other parishioners, and after the service I ran to the basement and stood at the edge of the table eating brown bread with butter and slices of ham. There were also buttery biscuits and jelly tarts. I drank five cups of milky tea.

When I got home Colin was dressed in his suit and tie, his face flushed as he told me a producer had called him, that the producer was casting a movie. He went out till past midnight and came home assuring me he'd get a part in the film and that all our money worries would be over. Every night he met the producer, always returning home long after midnight.

A few days later at the Bailey, Patsy recited Auden and the Diva quoted Nabokov.

"O what is the light I see flashing so clear," Patsy said.

The Diva cleared his throat and pressed his palm against his ascot. "TV's huge paperclip . . ."

After several drinks Patsy grew maudlin.

"It is the sorrow, shall it melt?"

"All colors make me happy," the Diva said unconvincingly. "Even gray."

I recited a few bars of John Denver's "Country Roads"

while Colin laid money on the table—he was late to meet his producer. Colson Dean came in and made his way directly to us.

"I can't meet at our regular time," he said to Colin.

All the domestic mysteries of my life aligned: Colin's recent physical aloofness, his mental preoccupation, his flushed features when he arrived home every night. I jumped up from the table and locked myself in the bathroom, where I kneeled down in front of the porcelain loo as if it were a statue of a saint. Ever since I first saw Colin, all I'd wanted was union with him. That union was impossible. "One has only the choice between God and idolatry," Simone Weil has written. "If one denies God . . . one is worshiping some things of this world in the belief that one sees them only as such, but in fact, though unknown to oneself imagining the attributes of Divinity in them." I decided to go home, and this thought darted around like a bat between the cool octagonal tiles and my hands resting in the folds of my skirt. The barman came to the door.

"Miss," he whispered, "I hear you crying in there, but God forgive me, a queue's forming and you need to come out of the loo."

CHAPTER 13

M Y FATHER WAS WAITING behind a metal partition as I came through customs at Kennedy airport. We drove toward Roanoke, stopping only once at a Shoney's. I stared at the huge laminated menu on the sticky orange tabletop and ordered from the bleach-blonde waitress who wore beige foundation makeup five times darker than her actual skin tone. All through dinner my father was oddly without affect, a blander version of his former self. He gave accounts of my brothers' activities. Jonathan was at soccer camp and David was working as a waiter. When I asked about my mom, he just shook his head.

As we drove deeper into the South, scrub pines banking the highway were covered with kudzu vines. When we finally pulled into our gravel drive, long past midnight, I saw my mother's face hanging moonlike in the dark kitchen window. She had lost weight and wore red lipstick. My father went straight to bed and my mother sat on the edge of the crate-furniture couch and asked me questions about Ireland. Like everything else I'd seen that day, the room with its pee-stained carpet and fake-wood paneling repulsed me. My digs in Ireland had been equally shabby, but with a certain aesthetic integrity. Even though it was hot, my mother had made my favorite: spaghetti and meatballs. She was eager to please me. A sheet cake with chocolate frosting sat on the black coils of the electric stove. She told me she'd been going to my dad's softball games, events she'd never much cared for before. Her eyes darted around the room and she played with a piece of paper, rolling it over her finger. She wasn't throwing around her misery anymore; now she was trying, wearing nail polish and plucking her eyebrows.

"Won't you have some food, honey?" my mother kept asking.

I knew the cake was a sort of peace offering. But I was already plotting my escape to the beach, where I'd waitressed the summer before. I was afraid if I took even a sliver of cake, I'd be stuck in that ranch house, in the purgatory of my parents' misery, forever.

Ocracoke Island, North Carolina, was still a remote fishing village in 1984 with a handful of hotels and a couple of restaurants. I lived with Vickie Cobb, a piano teacher from Charlotte who took in girls for the summer. We bunked two to a room in her run-down A-frame on the sound side of the island. I worked a combination of breakfast and dinner shifts at a restaurant and on the weekends at the island's only bar. For my breakfast shift, I got up in the dark and rode my bike with the wicker basket around the harbor. The water as the light rose was a mass of fractured color, lime green, navy, and lavender.

Most of the other waitresses were young mothers supplementing the income their husbands made fishing. I was intimidated by the integrity of their lives and acted aloof and superior. I was having trouble sleeping. I'd wake several times at night, thinking Colin's body was beside me. Sometimes after my shift, I would buy a little bottle of bourbon at the island's tiny liquor store, go out to the beach, and watch the waves.

The only person at the restaurant I felt any connection with was Roland. Roland, along with his boyfriend, ran a bed-and-breakfast called the Cruise Inn. It was one of the few gay-friendly places on the Carolina coast. Business was good but renovations were eating up profits and Roland was moonlighting at the restaurant. After our shift, while we set the tables for lunch, Roland told me that over the Fourth of July weekend, the house had been full of gay men wanting to party. Roland wore his brown hair short and his face was open and extremely expressive. He was in his early thirties but his demeanor was more like a teenager's. He wouldn't say exactly what had happened, just that things had gotten out of hand and that he felt bad about it. Really bad. The wake-up-in-the-night-with-your-heart-pounding kind of bad.

When the breakfast shift was over, I'd stay on to talk to him while he cleaned fish for the dinner special. The kitchen was white with chrome tables, refrigerator, and stove. Fish scales multiplied against the blade as he pulled the knife down the side of the flounder. He'd told me that since the Fourth, he'd been going to the island's Pentecostal church.

"I can't explain it," he said in his expansive Southern drawl. "It's like all of a sudden I feel somebody watching."

"You mean like Big Brother?"

"No, no," he said. "A friendly presence."

"Like an alien?"

"I know it sounds ridiculous. It's just so hard to explain!" he wailed in his campy way, and we both laughed.

I was skeptical. The religious students at my college had

been a badly dressed lot. I'd often see them when I was rushing to my early French class, huddled in a group and evoking Jesus's name. I'd also waited on the island's Pentecostal preacher. He spoke rhetorically even when ordering eggs and bacon and I couldn't believe he had any spiritual guidance for anybody. But I had to admit something was happening to my friend. After our dinner shift was over, we'd ride around in his Dodge Dart, cruise along the highway by the beach, and watch waves breaking up along the sand. Eventually we'd park down at the dock near the ranger station, and Roland would try to describe the sensation of his conversion.

"It's all this joy," he'd say, "just flowing out of my heart."

The dashboard lights were like the console of a spaceship as he told me he was noticing the bubbles that surrounded the fish in the fryers or the face of a little girl, her eyes the color of green sea glass. He knew God was trying to get his attention but he wasn't sure why. I went with him to visit two elderly African American ladies from his church. Both were homebound now, but they'd worked as maids at the island's big hotel. Roland bought them groceries and got up on a ladder to clean out the gutters of their one-room home. A sagging curtain separated the kitchen from the double bed, where they both slept.

"Roland is full of the spirit," the older lady told me. "You watch now what God is going to do."

I'd heard my father make fun of the woman in our church in Southington who claimed she'd seen a statue of Jesus lift his arms during her husband's funeral, and he rolled his eyes when anyone mentioned the Pentecostals. But I was interested and longed, though I wouldn't admit it even to myself, for a violent conversion.

On Wednesday evening I went with Roland and his boyfriend to the prayer service. The sanctuary was paneled with particle board and on the back wall was a paint-by-numbers portrait of Jesus. I recognized the cashier from the gas station, an older man who worked at the restaurant, and the ladies we'd visited. Roland sat between me and his boyfriend; he pointed out to us that the hymns that said CAMP MEETING were the most fun to sing. The liturgy consisted of simple statements of belief, and in the sermon the preacher laid out the rules like a gentle Little League coach: Without admitting to sin and being born again, there was no way into heaven. At the end of the sermon the preacher said Sister Linda would sing an original song. Linda worked as night clerk at the Island Inn. She was sixty and had long, wavy gray hair and a face wrinkled by sun exposure. The pianist began the intro and Linda sang about the red blood of the lamb turning black souls as white as snow. Each time she came around to the chorus, Roland squeezed my hand, which he'd taken in a brotherly way when the service first started.

Linda's song stripped religion down to its symbolic elements and imbued them with a mystical passion. The melody reminded me of the delicacy of the body and she sang in an honest, open way. After the song, the preacher showed us his bottle of oil, a small, old-fashioned-looking glass bottle with a red metal cap. My father always referred to the stuff as snake oil, and I was horrified when Roland slipped out of the pew and walked purposefully up to the altar, kneeling down to be anointed. The windows were all dark and the only light was from the fluorescent panels buzzing over our heads. The minister rubbed oil onto Roland's forehead. Roland fell over sideways and began to cry. His boyfriend, who wasn't a regular churchgoer, rolled his eyes and mumbled, "ridiculous." All this was a smoke screen, as far as he was concerned. If Roland wanted to leave him, well, fine, just be honest about it rather than making up a bunch of spiritual claptrap.

The following Sunday Roland and I rode over on the ferry to Nags Head for a revival in a church shaped like Noah's ark. The preacher had dark, wavy hair and a football player's charisma. His message focused on the things that keep us away from God. He seemed most concerned with women who watched soap operas and bought frozen food rather than cooking for their families. He worked himself up into a sweat, water dripping off his nose. Just after the sermon, a man spoke for a long time in what sounded like Hebrew scat. An older women offered an interpretation: "God wants us to obey." This seemed a little abbreviated; the man had spoken for at least three minutes, but the minister didn't seem upset by the translation's brevity. He announced that the holy spirit was in the place and that all those who wanted to be vehicles of the spirit should come up to the altar.

Roland bounded out of the pew and ran to the front. He was the first in a long line of people, and when the minister shouted into his face, he fell back and lay on the ground while an usher kneeled beside him praying. Finally he stood up and sheepishly made his way back.

"There was a word," he told me later as we waited for the ferry. "I felt it coming up, but before I could say it the word fell back down."

I identified with what he was saying, but not in a religious sense. It was the same when I tried to write. I was working on my first novel on a portable typewriter my mother had given me for Christmas and I could never communicate what I felt coming up. I was always disappointed with the sentences I wrote. They never conveyed the fullness of my initial idea.

Over the next month, at every altar call, Roland rushed up

the center aisle. Sometimes he fell over on the carpet. Other times he kneeled while others around him spoke in tongues. Once, when the minister dabbed oil on his forehead, I saw him open his lips in quick succession like a baby bird.

One night after our shift, as we drove around Silver Lake, he was quieter than usual.

"I asked the pastor why I can't get hold of the spirit," he said.

"And?"

"He says I'm not serious about my commitment to Christ."

"What does he want you to do? Join the priesthood?"

"He says I can't be gay anymore."

"But you're gay," I said. "That's how God made you."

"But am I gay?" he asked, raising one eyebrow.

We both laughed.

Soon after that night Roland told me he'd stopped sleeping with his boyfriend and in September he planned to leave the island and live with his mother in Tarboro, join the Pentecostal church, and find a nice woman to marry, preferably a divorcée with children.

Now when we rode around he talked about his future wife and kids, how they'd all go to church together and how he'd be a good father. His own father was dead, he had little contact with his brother, and his mother was only accepting him now that he was casting off his homosexuality.

In the last weeks of summer our shifts weren't in sync and Roland spent all his free time in church. I'd taken up with the bartender at the place I worked on weekends, a drifty computer major with a black mustache and a long white Cadillac Eldorado. Business during the weekend days was slow, and, more out of boredom than anything else, we'd been making out in the walk-in cooler, my back pressed up against the giant canisters of mayonnaise. The day I got a letter from Colin explaining that he and a friend of ours were moving together to Paris, I drank half a bottle of whiskey and in the evening, when I knew his shift was over, I walked to the rickety cottage the bartender shared with a prep cook and a lifeguard. Purple plastic beads hung over his doorway and Prince's "Purple Rain" played out from the glowing stereo console as we made out.

Within a few days I felt dizzy, my breasts sore against the nylon material of my bra. At work I forgot to bring people drinks and confused waffle orders with scrambled eggs. Every morning I ran to the toilet and gagged up bile, then watched the little islands float on the water's surface. There was no place to get a pregnancy test. I'd have to wait the two weeks until I got back to college, and then go to Planned Parenthood.

A few days before I left, Roland made me dinner in the empty restaurant after our shift. It was dark except for a candle fluttering on our table as we ate T-bone steaks with horseradish sauce and slices of tomato that Roland brought from his garden. Roland, who was usually jovial, seemed ill at ease. I wondered if he'd heard about me and the bartender. He kept staring into the flame at the center of the table. After a while he said he had something important to tell me. Finally, I thought, he's going back to his boyfriend and giving up all this born-again crap.

"You know I've been praying a lot."

"So you tell me," I said.

"Sometimes when I pray, your face comes up."

"Can't get me off your mind, huh?"

Roland remained serious. "I want you to come with me to Tarboro," he said. "I think we should live together."

I wondered if he'd guessed I was pregnant. I saw myself holding a baby, its small features pressed into my neck, but just as quickly the liminal crack sealed over. It was impossible. I was only twenty-one. I had to go back to college and finish my novel. I couldn't move to some podunk town, live with a born-again Christian gay man, and give birth to a baby. It was ludicrous.

I shook my head. "I'm flattered," I said, "but—"

"If it makes any difference to you, I've decided to become a minister," he said.

I shook my head. Roland told me he had sold back his part of the Cruise Inn and his mother said he could stay in the spare bedroom until he got an apartment.

The night I left the island I packed my clothes, my books, and my little typewriter into my trunk, set it by the doorway, and rode my bike over to the restaurant. I was taking the first ferry off the island in the morning. The restaurant kitchen was chaotic with activity. I saw Roland pulling a rack of pots out of the dishwasher and steam encasing his upper body. He smiled when he saw me and told me to wait in the yard. I stood next to a boxwood bush, pulled a saltine out of my pocket, and bit off the edge; crackers were the only thing that fought off my nausea. The screen door slammed as Roland stepped outside wearing his kitchen whites, his hair smoothed down. He took my hand and closed his eyes.

"Lord, bless Darcey," he said. "Keep her safe, keep her from evil, keep her eyes on the lamb and lead her ever forward. Watch over her and bring her closer to your light."

Years later Roland would call me from Key West, where he'd decamped after a disastrous marriage and acrimonious divorce.

CHAPTER 14

T HE PLANNED PARENTHOOD OFFICE sat in a strip mall between a hairdresser supply shop and a Christian book store. In the waiting room two teenage girls sat whispering to each other. A middle-aged lady read a magazine. The receptionist called my name and a nurse walked me down the carpeted corridor to the procedure room. I wore a blue sweater with a white yoke and khaki shorts, and the nurse asked if I was a preppy. *The Preppy Handbook* was still popular and references to preppies and the British equivalent, Sloan Rangers, were everywhere in the news. Before I could answer, she said, "I'm going to call you Preppy."

During the abortion I kept my head turned sideways, my cheek pressed against the paper sheet, my hand grasping the nurse's. Blue veins throbbed in the fleshy part of my thumb; each tendon articulated itself in my wrist.

Under her unpolished nails the nurse's skin was lavender.

"How you doing, Preppy?" she said over the whirr of the vacuum.

When it was over and I'd rested the requisite half hour, my

legs loose beneath me, I walked out the side door and over to the phone booth near the Hallmark store and called the cab company. I felt, as I waited on the curb, as if I'd died and my diaphanous self floated over the asphalt. I was light-headed, sick to my stomach. It felt like a piece of the metal rod had broken off and was sitting cold and implacable inside my uterus. I spread my knees and threw up. When I looked up a man sitting in a delivery truck was staring down at me. At first I thought he was laughing, his eyes bright under his baseball cap, but when he rolled down his window I felt a burst of air-conditioning and he asked if I needed any help.

I shook my head and stood; my cab was pulling into the lot. I saw that the cab driver was the same one who talked all the way there about how his wife had left him. His cab was a shrine to his former family. He'd even glued one of his daughter's teddy bears over the radio. I sat gingerly in the backseat and was relieved that for now the man was quiet. He'd probably picked up other pale, woozy girls in the Planned Parenthood parking lot. I rolled down the window and let warm air collide against my face. Other than that moment with Roland, I'd never let myself think of the heaviness I felt in my uterus as being a baby. I'd imagined the fetus more like a larva with a rubbery doll's face. But debasing the life inside me didn't do much to assuage the sorrow I felt as the cab merged onto the interstate.

In the weeks after the abortion, while I was eating in the college cafeteria or waiting for my clothes to dry in the laundry room, I'd think about buying a gun. The gun-shop owner would make jokes about a girl like me needing firearms, and I'd hide the gun between my box spring and mattress in my dorm room. I'd put on a raw linen dress with big malachite buttons, the only one left from my mother's pageant days. No matter how cold it was, I'd walk into the woods that surrounded the campus. I'd lean against a big rock in a fairy circle of maples, unzip my bag, and stare down at the gun lying at the bottom among pens and scraps of paper. I played the scenario over and over until it drove out all other thoughts and I became like a robotic insect, waking, dressing, moving down the hall toward the cafeteria, where I watched Cheerios fall from the plastic dispenser into my bowl.

One Sunday during this time I went to chapel, first to the morning service, where the college chaplain gave a sermon about world hunger. In the evening I went to Catholic mass. The priest's face was red and I saw that his black suit had flecks of dandruff spread over his lapels as I kneeled down to receive the chalice. When I got home I lay in bed and thought about slipping the dress on and heading into the woods. I was half asleep when I heard the girls on my hall yelling, "Darcey, look out the window!" I dragged my body up and pulled back the curtain. A hot air balloon hovered over the quad, right next to my dorm. The billowing cloth was striped red, orange, and yellow, and the wicker basket was swinging gently as the flame receded and the balloon drifted down below the tree line. I threw open the wrought iron frame and leaned out. The man in the basket was so near I could see his reddish beard stubble and make out that his wire-rimmed glasses were bifocals.

"Which way to Orioles Stadium?" he shouted.

I pointed toward downtown Baltimore.

"Thank you," he said, tipping his head first at me and then at all the girls hanging out of the dorm windows waving. He pulled a rope with a gloved hand and a flame shot up into the balloon, heating the air. As his basket rose, the balloon was illuminated by the last rays of the sun.

CHAPTER 15

I N 1988 I CAME to live in my father's rectory on Maujer Street in the Williamsburg section of Brooklyn. My father had left my mom and taken a job as a chaplain at New York University Medical Center, and on Sundays he preached at St. John's Lutheran. Plaster fell down in patches from the rectory's high ceiling, and it wasn't unusual to see paint chips lying around on the gray institutional carpet. Dad had just broken off his rebound relationship with Susan, an intense middle-aged woman with thick glasses and short hair. She was the leader of her building's civilian police project. I remember one torturous dinner during which she detailed to my father and me the variations of violence she was allowed, as a civilian representative of the law, to unleash on intruders: karate, pepper spray, handcuffs.

I'd come from San Francisco, where I'd left behind a string of disastrous relationships. Boyfriends had overlapped. Boyfriends became entrenched inside relationships with other boyfriends. Boyfriends would not take hints and therefore I would take flight. Boyfriends held me in what felt like a death grip. While I had affection for them, I was also in a transitory place, not really able to single out any one boyfriend for a forever-type relationship. My problem was one of cowardice. I couldn't tell them I was ambivalent. Instead I pretended that I was in woozy deep love with each of them and I'd hint that one day, far in the future, there was the possibility of cohabitation, even marriage.

My parents had split up over the weekend of my college graduation a few years before, and my mother served my father divorce papers at my graduation from graduate school at the University of Virginia. My mother, who was still in the Virginia ranch house, said she wouldn't have had children if she'd known how things would turn out and called my father a slimebag and a psychopath. She hated, among other things, tacky window-unit air conditioners and the fact that vocational students graduated in cap and gown. Also the heat. She got visibly agitated when the temperature rose above 75 degrees. "I hate the heat," she'd say twenty times in a single afternoon, her face deeply tormented as if the heat were attacking her directly. My mother was particularly bitter about religion. She told me many times that when she'd had her nervous breakdown, her therapist told her that my father was a "Peter Pan man" and that "the world has no place for men who believe in angels." She felt all ministers were frauds and that church was a sham. She told me once again how as a little girl in Albany she'd joined my grandfather's church by herself, how he'd confirmed her, and how she'd assumed that the minister's son, my father, would be a quality person, not a charlatan.

In the Williamsburg rectory I lived in one of the upstairs bedrooms with cloudy, curtainless windows and cracked linoleum floors. On Sundays I'd go next door to hear my father preach. He'd recently told me sheepishly that, after years of disillusionment, he'd been reunited with the church. The sanctuary was red brick with high ceilings. The stained glass windows were patched with chicken wire. Many of the current parishioners had come in the sixties as college kids to work on social programs and never left. Richard John Neuhaus became the minister at St. John's in 1961 and throughout the sixties the church was a mecca for both liturgical reform and political action. Neuhaus was the liaison for Martin Luther King Jr. in New York state and the organizer of church events like the Independence Day antiwar fast and a draft-card-burning ceremony, where young men were encouraged to turn in their cards at the altar while the congregation sang "America the Beautiful." Clergy and Laymen Concerned About Vietnam, the group that had sponsored the post office events we went to in Southington, was started in the church basement by Rabbi Abraham Joseph Heschel, Reverend Neuhaus, and Father Daniel Berrigan. Both Ralph Abernathy, King's successor, and Coretta Scott King spoke at St. John's after King's death.

Unfortunately the congregation's glory days were past; Church break-ins weren't unusual. I came home once to find the safe door open, the collection money gone, and a pile of feces on the blotter of my father's desk. Sunday services were scattered, disorganized affairs. The organist played dramatically no matter how few people were in the pews. Often my father had to wait several minutes for the reader to find the Bible verse or for the choir to sing. A tiny Hispanic man named Raul read the announcements, always including events at every church in a fifty-block radius and then praising God till my father had to take control of the podium and cut him off.

When I was a child I loved to hear my father preach. Sometimes he used stories about our family life. Other times he used pop songs like "Bridge over Troubled Water" or "I Want to Hold Your Hand" to illustrate a point. Often he used props: a fat seventies tie versus a skinny fifties one. But my Sundays of sitting in rapture were over. Ever since my parents broke up, the last thing I wanted to do was to hear my dad's sermons.

Now his messages focused on the group he ran for men with AIDS at the Gay Men's Health Crisis Center. He'd detail the death tableau: the emaciated young man, his face glowing as sisters, brothers, mom, and dad all stood around gently weeping. "You were a good boy, Richie," the father, holding the hand of his son, said. "You were a good dad," said Richie. I sat in the pew, the cold wood against my back, and I wanted to jump out of my skin. Now that my family was dismantled, I couldn't stand that my father was supporting other families in their most intimate moments.

Because I was new to the city, I was still easily startled by the garbage trucks grinding at three a.m. and the hostile voices on the street. My hands were always grimy and my shoulders hunched as I walked down our block past the brownstones with boarded windows and stairwells piled high with trash. The man who worked the cash register at the bodega on the corner had only one arm, and most of his customers bought pints of beer and lottery tickets.

The only person I knew in New York was Michael. We met a few times while I'd lived in San Francisco and talked about surrealist films and house music. He'd come back east to get his film certificate from NYU and now he was recording an album with his band Ajax for the industrial dance music label Wax Trax. When we met in Manhattan at a health food restaurant, he told me his mother and father were Midwestern squares and hard-core Republicans. They disapproved of his bohemian lifestyle and had refused to pay his college tuition. Even in his black jeans, motorcycle jacket, and adorable velvet porkpie hat, I saw how his frame grew brittle as he talked about his parents. He'd worked his way through school and was now bartending. While I was already attracted to Michael, his parents' disapproval was like an aphrodisiac. I was amazed he hadn't let their negation get to him. He had cultivated a cynical remove, a sort of unconcerned demeanor that I wanted for myself. We went, after dinner, for drinks at Spring Street Bar, and while we drank bourbon and talked, a white poodle in a red calico dress and handkerchief came in with her owner.

That night Michael stayed over at the rectory. We'd just fallen asleep around four a.m. when I heard my dad calling me from the stairwell. I pulled on my jeans and sweatshirt and walked to the top of the stairs. My father's round face was creased with worry as he asked me if there was somebody up there named Michael.

"Shit," Michael said as he stood up and pulled on his jeans.

"Yeah, Dad, there is."

"Well, there's a call for him," my dad said. "Can he answer the phone up there in the kitchen?"

Michael was already picking up the phone in the dark kitchen.

"I can't come home."

Pause.

"I'm not coming home."

Pause.

"I'm in the middle of Brooklyn. I can't leave now."

Pause.

"I told you."

I realized the woman he shared an apartment with was not simply his roommate, as he'd led me to believe. Finally he hung up the phone, came in, and lay down beside me. The phone started to ring again, I heard my dad's footsteps downstairs in the hall.

"Darce," he called. "Darcey!"

Michael buttoned his jeans back up and picked up the phone. I heard him say he'd come, he'd have to wait for the subway, but he'd come home. I walked him down to the front door. He kissed me and said he'd explain everything later. I let him out and watched him run down the steps in his Prince Valiant haircut and Doc Martens. When I turned I saw that my father's reading light was on. I thought I was in for a lecture, one I clearly deserved, but my father just read his book, his hand pale against the illuminated page.

Things moved fast. Michael moved out and got a loft in Chinatown with a drag queen, a DJ, and a couple of goth teenagers. The teenagers, Clare and Andy, always wore black lipstick and looked like the children from *The Addams Family*. Miss Hogg, otherwise known as Dean, did secretarial work in the day and at night performed at dance clubs.

Miss Hogg would burst into Michael's room in the middle of the night wearing a nurse's uniform, a blonde wig, a full face of makeup, and a pig snout. The way she stomped around frightened me, but I was also drawn to her dark drama. When she performed, Miss Hogg worked herself up into a frenzy of insatiable appetite. Her face contorted as the strobe light beat faster. In the white light she looked demonic, her hair aflame, blue glitter on her eyelids, the latex snout looking like a natural part of her bovine features.

Miss Hogg often threatened to come out to Brooklyn and break into my father's Sunday service. I imagined her drinking the communion wine and gobbling all the wafers. Rather than advocating Christ's message of forgiveness, Miss Hogg was an avatar of rage and excess, qualities that fascinated me.

Though my hours were odd now, I still pulled myself out of bed when I heard my dad call me to church Sunday mornings. *Darce, Darcey, are you coming to church?* The church people had been nice enough to let me live rent-free in the rectory, but my father knew, as I did, that the only requisite was that I go to Sunday services. Michael was also raised Lutheran. Now he was an atheist and found religion ridiculous. To please me he came to services a few times, sullen in his punk-rock plaid pants as he sang under his breath, "Holy holy moly Jesus is a phony!" The first big fight we had was about going to church. "If you make me go every Sunday," he told me, "we have to break up."

My father was spending most of his time at his new girlfriend's house. He slept at Anne's every night she didn't have her kids, and even when she had her two boys he went over for dinner. The first time I saw Anne was on a Saturday afternoon. I used my key to get in and as I walked through the living room, a young woman rushed past me in a skirt and white bra. She pressed her blouse over her chest, ran into the bathroom at the end of the hallway, and slammed the door.

My father sat slouched in the corner, his blue oxford unbuttoned and his large Germanic face flushed with make-out endorphins. His honey-blond hair was disheveled, strands tufted up like a cockateel's feathers.

"You need to knock before you come in," he told me.

Dad looked embarrassed as he buttoned up his shirt and readjusted the pillows on the couch. I was startled but not that much. During this time, after my dad left my mom, he was often either dazed or manic. He'd grown up on Long Island and had always longed to live in New York City. On my first visit earlier in the year, he'd taken me to an expensive French restaurant; the entrées costed five times what I was used to and I felt uncomfortable knowing that my mother was down in Virginia eating Hamburger Helper. He gave me a buffalo plaid shirt, saying with big city authority that buffalo plaid had replaced paisley, though he must have seen I was wearing paisley jeans.

The night after I surprised Dad and Anne on the couch, they made dinner for me. As we ate acorn squash stuffed with smoked mozzarella, Dad chattered nervously about the little Italian man in the white apron who had smoked the cheese right on the sidewalk in front of his shop. My dad loved New York City. According to him, everything was better in Manhattan. The pizza and the bread were better, people were smarter and better dressed, the espresso was fantastic! Every conversation that night funneled into New York's excellence. Anne was part of New York's grandeur. She'd gone to Smith College and was now studying at General Seminary to be an Episcopal priest. She wore a dark A-line dress, her blonde hair pulled into a low ponytail and fastened with a tortoiseshell clip. Her symmetrical features were beautiful, though the set of her mouth—the corners turned down—made her look sullen and unhappy.

After my father got back from walking Anne to the subway, he told me more intimate details about her. Her younger sister had run away, married a drug dealer, and been shot to death in a park in Texas. A conversion experience had followed. As Anne lay in the bathtub, the window darkened and the ceiling filled with glittery light. A voice, like her voice but more authoritative, said, "I too have been pierced." After this experience, my father said, she began to attend an Episcopal church and eventually decided to go to seminary.

My dad's face was radiant as he spoke about Anne. He'd already mythologized details of her life and I knew he was in love. When he announced, not long after, that they were getting married, I was concerned. Dad hadn't been alone at all since he left my mom. He was charming and charismatic, but his enthusiasms were maniacal. An idea grabbed hold of him: the supremacy of New York City, Alice Miller's theory of trauma, Bettelheim's view of forgiveness. All conversational roads would lead to this topic. It was hard to get his attention unless, like one of his patients, you were recovering from open-heart surgery. Preoccupation was his defining quality; a sort of blankness often overtook him. As teenagers, behind his back, we'd called him the Lunch Box.

Lights on but nobody home, my brothers and I would whisper to one another as we watched him space out and float into another room.

On Saturday nights, while the choir practiced and the low tones of the organ vibrated through the alley and into my rectory bedroom, Michael and I took our disco naps. When we woke the stained glass window outside my own was prismatic with burgundy, gold, and violet blue, and we'd dress for the club. After a long stretch of dormancy my attraction to glamour was reviving. Near the end of college I'd given up wearing makeup, and in graduate school I kept my hair in a messy ponytail and wore thrift-store dresses. In committing myself to literature, I believed I had to abandon my former devotion to glamour. For a while my fashion icons were writers, Virginia Woolf and Marguerite Duras. I was more interested in

137

looking intelligent than pretty. Now Michael advised me to throw out my gauze skirts and shabby dresses in favor of bell-bottoms and Doc Martens boots.

At midnight we rode the L train into Manhattan. People mobbed the entrance of Mars, straining against the velvet rope. Club kids, exotic as zoo animals, arrived in taxis. Once I saw James St. James in a leopard-skin bodysuit and gold platform tennis shoes. With him was a girl wearing a blue taffeta baby-doll dress, white electrical tape arranged on her face like tribal markings. The crowd parted for its royalty. Michael stood beside me in faux complacency, but I could feel the tension in his body. To be noticed meant a lot to him. Eventually the door diva, Miss Julie, would see us and motion us through. Mark Kamins, who was producing Michael's single, "Mind the Gap," was deejaying, so we were usually on the guest list.

The walls of Mars's main dance floor were covered with hubcaps. A boy with rainbow eyelashes, his face covered with pink glitter, was kissing a being in a red yarn wig and purple pancake makeup. I was often on Ecstasy, the white powder that at first made my heart pound noisily against my chest but then bloomed out until my soul seemed to surround my body and extend out onto the dance floor. I loved *everyone*! I thought life was fantastic! Everyone was my friend! At Mars I felt I had escaped the regimentation of modern life and that, along with my fellow seekers, I had returned to a tribal utopia. The music, bass-line heavy and disorienting, rose above my head and I was pulled under. Kamins, Michael's producer, often wore beads and a sort of tunic like an Indian chieftain. The girl next to me had eyebrows shaped like rectangles and was completely bald. Her boyfriend wore a black net tank top and a wig made of rubber gloves.

At the Limelight, in an old church on Twenty-fourth Street, young women in thongs, their bodies greased and shimmering, danced in metal cages suspended over the altar. I'd feel myself drawn toward a darkness I'd always felt but was never able to articulate. I thought of the charcoal briquettes in our backyard grill. Long after the hamburgers were eaten, I'd come out to stare at the glowing embers. The boy in the fake-blood-splattered dress and the girl in the candy-colored wig and six-inch eyelashes were projections of God. Not the God of my childhood but a raw God, crude but also beautiful.

One Sunday my brothers arrived from college for a family meeting. We took Dad to a restaurant under the Brooklyn Bridge. Paper ferns hung from the ceiling and the trees outside were covered with bee lights.

After we ordered I began.

"We brought you here to talk to you."

Dad folded his hands in his lap, his elbows hanging over the sides of the chair. He smiled hard and was clearly uncomfortable.

"Shoot," he said.

"We all like Anne," I began, "but don't you think a little more time—"

"Not really," my father interrupted. "I love Anne and we want to be together."

Jonathan sighed loudly. "What about Looney Susan with her nunchuks and police batons? You were crazy about her too."

Dad's face reddened. "There is no comparison between Anne and Susan."

"Dad," David began. He was getting a degree in psychology and was good at reasoning with him. "Anne's divorce just came through. Don't you want to hold off a little?"

Dad looked into each of our faces with barely disguised frustration. He had a disorienting ability to move on, to flee the past and live entirely in the present. Whenever we talked about our childhoods, particularly around Anne, his expression became disapproving and he seemed frantic to change the subject.

"No," he said firmly, "we're going to get married. I don't like being alone that much."

Our salads came and his hand shook as he tipped the silver cup of dressing over the romaine lettuce.

The night Michael's single "Mind the Gap" came out, we went to Mars. Miss Hogg was there in her snout and French maid's uniform as was Pierre, a guy from the record label who was staying with us. Pierre's head was shaved except for a single lock that fell over his forehead. He had full lips and gray eyes. He was French and told us in heavily accented English that he wanted to live in Disney World. He wanted his address to be: Pierre, Disney World. The day he arrived, his suitcase covered with band stickers, we'd eaten ramen noodles together. Since then I hadn't seen him much. Michael was in the deejay booth as "Mind the Gap" came on. A girl in an aqua minidress and white go-go boots swung her mane of synthetic hair, and a tiny bald man in black, whom I later found out was Moby—the electronic recording artist—danced like an electrified atom. Miss Hogg swayed her substantial bottom and hit nearby dancers with her feather duster.

I wanted to dance with the drag queen Connie Girl.

Over many Saturday nights I had watched her in her waiflike disco outfits—sequined tube tops and latex stretch pants—dancing with her Puerto Rican boyfriend. I had been raised on images of the smooth-bodied, flowing-haired Jesus

as well as told, before I could even speak, that a guardian angel hovered, sparkly and dreamy-eyed, below the ceiling of
my bedroom. So I was particularly susceptible to Connie
Girl's thin shoulders and glittery makeup. It wasn't only her
glamour that affected me but also her singular sadness; she
seemed homesick for her own planet.

I asked her to dance and to my surprise she said yes. As we
took the dance floor, the mirror ball sent out little leaflets of
light. Connie Girl didn't move much, but strands of her hair
swayed around her face like a seductive veil and I felt mesmerized by her transitory image as it shifted from girl to boy.
My mind could not place her within its preestablished in- or
out-boxes, so Connie Girl hovered in that limbo, neither man
nor woman but a protean being with high teacup breasts and
shapely teenage-boy biceps.

I can't remember how Michael and I got home that night.
We probably took the subway, but if we had enough money
between us we might have taken a cab to the rectory. What
I do remember is hearing my dad's voice in the morning:
"Darce, Darcey." I got up, pulled on my clothes, and walked
into the kitchen. There was Pierre, who must have let himself
in sometime during the night, sitting at the table, a syringe
clenched between his teeth and a shoelace tied around his bi-
cep. He slapped the wormy inside of his arm looking for a
vein.

"Darcey," my father called. "Are you up there?"

I ran to the top of the stairwell. My father's face was
creased with fine wrinkles; he looked worried. He and Anne
were fighting a lot, and, while he adored her, I could see already that they were going to be miserable together.

"Are you coming over to church?"

I nodded. "Yeah. I'll be there in just a minute."

I watched my dad lock the two dead bolts and shuffle down the brownstone steps.

Back in the kitchen Pierre dropped the needle and fell forward, his cheek resting on the table, his eyelids sunk to show just a sliver of white.

PART FOUR

CHAPTER 16

IN THE SPRING OF 1993, *Spin* magazine asked me to cover the standoff in Texas between the Branch Davidians and the ATF. By this time I'd published two novels and was making a living as a writer. I arrived in Waco on the twenty-eighth day of the siege. Fifty cars, twenty campers, fifteen satellite trucks, and a dozen white tents lined the country road that led to the compound. The biggest tents, closest to the Department of Public Safety checkpoint, housed newscasters from the networks. Magazine journalists like myself sat around in lawn chairs soaking up the spring sun. After a few hours at the press site, I'd check out the siege sideshow. Vendors sold David Koresh T-shirts and Mount Carmel teddy bears. Young entrepreneurs sold soft drinks out of ice-filled coolers, and an older man had fired up a grill and sold barbecued chicken and ribs.

I felt superior to the Branch Davidians, who, as far as I was concerned, were naïve souls swayed by a madman. I was drawn to the story's tabloid elements: Koresh's alleged relationship with underage girls, his stockpiled guns, his claim to be the messiah. It was kitsch of the highest order. I interviewed local rock 'n' roll musicians who'd jammed with Koresh back in the days when the future cult leader had been a Spinal Tap–esque heavy metal guitarist. "This whole thing definitely had to do with thwarted musical ambition," one music store owner told me. "He couldn't be a rock star, so he decided to be Jesus. That was his vibe—a very misunderstood savior."

Even the press conferences were perversely humorous. A tabloid reporter asked how Koresh kept so many wives satisfied, and more than once an ATF spokesperson reported that some mixed-up kid had broken *into* the compound. Late in the siege a couple of reporters threw a party at the press site. In the distance Mount Carmel looked like a pink storybook castle. Spotlights shone all night into the windows, and the ATF blasted the sounds of rabbits being slaughtered. At the party the DPS guys gave out get-off-free speeding coupons and I drank beer and danced on a patch of grass between two trailers.

The day after the party, I was lying out in my lawn chair eating Mexican takeout and drinking a Diet Coke. It was mid-April, still chilly in New York, and I was happy to be sitting in the Texas sun.

"VAN!" someone shouted, and the cameramen and photographers jumped up from their chairs and pointed their lenses at the checkpoint.

Reporters burst out of their tents and trailers in flip-flops and baseball caps. I left my lunch and moved with the others to the edge of the asphalt, supposing I'd see yet another sullen Davidian looking vehemently out the front window. I was mistaken. Behind the van's tinted glass was a little girl, her feet jutted over the edge of the vinyl seat, tennis shoes dangling.

146

Though the weather was warm, she wore a snowsuit, the fur-edged hood covering her head. As I pressed up to the window, the girl turned her face to me. She'd been told about the godless people outside the compound and she was frightened to see us close up. Beside her a female agent held a baby. The reporters ran back to their trailers. If Koresh was letting out children, the siege might be turning violent.

I walked back to my lawn chair and continued eating my lunch, watching a television guy step onto a box, his short black hair so perfectly groomed it looked like plastic. A bearded man in jeans and work boots pointed the camera at his face and his mouth began to move, though he was too far away for me to hear what he was saying. These cultists, I realized, weren't comic-book characters. Extreme as they might seem to outsiders, the Davidians were committed to a practice that was meant to satisfy their spiritual hunger. If they had been led astray by David Koresh, it had been because they'd been desperately seeking to fill a spiritual longing, one not that dissimilar from the longing that, at the time, I couldn't admit existed within myself.

I was typing at my desk back in Brooklyn the afternoon the fifty-one-day siege came to an end. I flipped on the television and saw footage of the pink compound encased in flames and tendrils of whirling smoke. The siege's violent climax left eighty-seven Branch Davidians dead. Seventeen of them were children.

In the months after I returned from Waco my grandmother—my mother's mother—was diagnosed with cancer. I rode the train up once a week to visit her in Albany. She lay in St. Peter's Hospital watching television and eating Popsicles. She was tipsy and girlish when doped on morphine, but between doses her face blanched pink-white and I could tell she was in pain. Her parents had worked for a wealthy family, her mother as a housekeeper and her father as a chauffeur. Both had died before she was seven and she was raised by her mother's cousin. As a young woman she dated Chip Corning, the mayor's son. He took her to his family's box at the track in Saratoga and to fancy house parties up at Warner's Lake. Mayor Corning didn't approve of my grandmother's humble origins. He broke up the relationship, and on the rebound my grandmother married my grandfather and lived a simple life with him: He worked as a bakery-truck driver and she as a medical assistant. Still, she never lost her attraction to the trappings of luxury that she developed from being raised around a wealthy family and dating a rich boy. She was obsessed with Queen Elizabeth's jewels and owned several picture books on the subject. When the queen appeared on television my grandmother would tell me that the emerald diadem was known as the Delhi Dunbar Parure, or that the huge sapphire pin was the Prince Albert Brooch. Even as I rolled her around the hospital ward, she greeted nurses with a sort of high society formality. Every time I visited, she was weaker and more girlish. Just before they moved her to hospice, she made me roll her to the end of the hallway to see if another patient had any candy left in the box his daughter had left the day before.

The last time I saw my grandmother was on a Sunday evening. My mother waited in the car outside the hospital while I said good-bye. She thrashed around, saying she wanted to go home. She asked for her mother and called me Paige, my own mother's name. A tape played the sound of water falling and I touched my grandmother's arm, her skin powdery and loose. Her brown eyes were liquid like the soft caramel candies she loved. Her hand moved into mine and she gazed over the top of my head, smiling as tiny babies will sometimes do.

After the funeral, as the train raced toward New York City, I thought about my grandmother and I thought about God. I remember once seeing my grandfather kneel beside his bed and say the Lord's Prayer. My grandmother didn't attend church, but when my grandfather died she found a minister to officiate at his funeral. That January was one of the coldest on record. Out the window I watched the frozen Hudson, smoky patches of ice, and, occasionally, where the ice was broken, angles of navy-blue water. When darkness fell, the temperature dropped and the train doors froze shut. When the train stopped in Poughkeepsie a man in a thermal suit came out of the station with a blowtorch. The purple flame in the dark threw a raspberry patina over the snow, and I realized I was hoping that my grandmother had tried to get to know God. I hoped so insistently that my hope turned into a prayer.

After my grandmother died I was spacey and forgetful, locking myself out of my apartment or staring intently at the ground turkey, mottled pink and white, in the refrigerator. One of our paintings of a man in a torture device upset me so much that I'd cover it with a scarf as soon as Michael left for work in the morning. In my dreams a lady in a red sweater was trying to tell me something, but I couldn't make out the features of her blurry face. In another the lake beyond the house was deep and black, its boundaries indistinguishable from the shore. When I woke, my teeth were always clenched. In the evening Michael brought home thrift-store records. After dinner he'd take out his rolling papers and want me to smoke with him. I sat on our thrift-store couch surrounded by Jesus art while he deejayed for me, holding the headphones up to his ears and cuing up records. His pupils as big as dimes and his cheeks flushed, Michael was extremely animated.

After talking about how corporations like Microsoft ran the government, and how because of pollution the earth would soon implode, he'd always come back to his life as a small-time rock star in Portland, Oregon, where he'd moved after high school. The rainy city with its funky wooden Victorians still haunted him with its lush dampness, the moss growing on the roof and mushrooms springing up at the base of the bathtub. The stories were like the Stations of the Cross. Each one held something sacramental for him: how after his band played, he'd made out with two girls backstage; how he often rigged up electricity in abandoned buildings for concerts; how for a while he lived in his van, using the bathroom of the local coffeehouse. Michael cued up an early Percy Sledge record, a cool thrift-store find. The light from the angel lamp showed the grain of the velvet shade, and the Keane Kid's haunted eyes reminded me of the Branch Davidian girl. I felt as disconnected as a dust mote, careening around in a shaft of light.

I figured only saints and mystics got to feel God. I wanted something more tangible, a liberal theology and a manageable practice that would help me deal with my anxiety and make me a better person. I squinted over catalogs for the Omega Center, wondering if Tantric Centering Prayer, Power Healing, or Shang-Lo Yoga would help me. I fantasized that I'd find a teacher, a guru, a man in a black turtleneck with a well-trimmed beard and small wire-rimmed glasses, who would convey to me the secret of life.

My soul, long dormant, had woken and was starving, crying out like a famished infant. But I was as unprepared for the task of integrating my own pain into my life as I was in truly engaging in any religious work. I bought a book on Zen meditation and went to yoga classes at the Energy Center. Afterward I read over the signs on the bulletin board: Hindu life coaching, rolfing, tantric healers, hypnotists, chanting sessions. I peeled off all the telephone numbers, knowing I'd never call any of them.

Sometimes I'd talk to Anne, my new stepmother. Anne worked for the bishop at St. John the Divine, helping to select potential priests for the ordination process as well as staffing the committee that disciplined wayward priests. There was the priest who had grown paranoid and stockpiled guns in the church safe; Anne, along with a phalanx of police officers, went out to confront him. There was the priest who'd brought over a young Brazilian love slave. Lesser infractions were common: married priests sleeping with parishioners, priests skimming money off the collection plate. Anne wore a leather jacket over her black shirt and white clerical. She looked impossibly cool, like a divine version of *Get Smart's* Agent 99. Once, when a defrocked priest was stalking her, she had to stay in a safe house. Her sermons so affected me that I'd ask for copies. In one she used the Mary and Martha story to explain how people sometimes use their talents to keep others away. "I am certain that in each of our lives God is inviting us to a deeper and more satisfying kind of attachment and way of relating to each other," she wrote, "a way not marked by approval-seeking and impressiveness but by a kind of no-strings-attached generosity in which what we can do for each other is not as important as who we are for each other."

After reading a profile of the New Age mystic Andrew Harvey in the *New York Times Magazine*, I went to hear him talk. I'd read his book *Hidden Journey*, and while I wasn't con-vinced the young Indian avatar Mother Meera was actually divine, I was convinced of Harvey's devotion to her. Expecta-tions were high among the mostly middle-aged crowd of women in dangly earrings and men in comfortable sweaters. Harvey, his long, wavy hair falling to his collar, sat on a raised wooden chair and spoke about grace. We have natural grace as children, but we lose it in adolescence. All religions, Har-vey claimed, were attempts to reestablish this wonder and grace. His final precepts—to love one another, to love oneself, to respect the earth—were ideas familiar to me from Sunday school.

For a few days after I'd think about Harvey's gleaming hair, so black it glinted blue, and the passionate way he moved his hands. I wanted to feel a kinship to him, but he was more glamorous than inspirational; there was no sign that he felt broken in the deep way that I did.

CHAPTER 17

I SAT ON THE edge of my bed, the thermometer in my mouth, looking down at the graph paper with rows of temperature readings. The ovulation chart, the thermometer with the red vein: These were holy implements. I no longer went to classes at the Open Center or read books on cultivating inner light. Now my mind had two modes. The most common was worry that I couldn't get pregnant, which manifested itself as a sort of pulsing in my brain that knocked out coherent thought. The other was ecstasy as I imagined the soft skin and warm, loose belly of a baby. I studied books on fertility, how having sex with the lights on stimulated ovulation, how nettle and rose hip widened the cervix.

In every conversation I wanted to blurt out, "I am dying to get pregnant!" A tiny, spooky hand often motioned to me from the netherworld. I became obsessed with my body, every twinge making me wonder if an egg was moving down the fallopian tube, if the lining of my uterus was thickening with blood. I would watch my feet and bare ankles as I walked down Montague Street, how my knees looked as I sat on the little velvet couch in the living room. I'd stare at the blonde hairs on my arms. It wasn't that I thought I was some sort of fertility goddess. I was horrified by my skinny white limbs and my greasy features. I looked at my face in the bathroom mirror. Was this the face of somebody whom God would entrust with a baby? I'd killed the first baby I'd been given. Why should I be given another? A pagan thought, but there I was, watching my feet on the sidewalk. The delicacy of the tendons made clear my fragile predicament. The phrase "At God's mercy" was fully rendered.

As I got ready for bed the night before my daughter was born, a few drops of cloudy water fell down from between my legs. Five ragged circles, the consistency of skim milk. I studied them; I was four weeks away from my due date and didn't think it was possible that my water could have broken. I mentioned the possibility to Michael. He assured me I had several weeks to go. When the lights were out I felt blood beat through my body, pounding as it surged to my hands and feet. My baby began, as she did every evening, to hiccup against my pelvis. It was not an unpleasant sensation, rhythmic, even melodic, and it soothed me into sleep and one vivid technicolor image after another. The dreams had different characters and surreal plot twists, but what was consistent was the long expanse of bright green grass. I saw each blade in detail and the blue sky was like stained glass. When I opened my bedroom closet in one dream, I found grass growing over my shoes.

By seven the next evening I was howling. Neighbors came out of their apartments to see who was being murdered as I waited for the elevator. In the taxi, which was driven by a man with a black beard and a white turban, I continued to scream. Pain wore away my identity so that I felt the same as the air, the leather car seat, the trees outside the window. The aura around every streetlight was mealy and the blue-black night oozy like oil, inking the car as we rushed toward the hospital.

"Is there anything to do?" I saw the driver's brown eyes in the slice of rearview mirror.

The midwife shook her head. She wore a quilted Indian-print jacket and socks with her Birkenstocks. Her full face was placid, not uncaring, but peaceful. It was as if she were in the cab by herself on the way to a dinner party. Holding Michael's hand on one side and the midwife's on the other, I writhed in the moving cab. I felt my pelvis edging open and my consciousness, as if made of paper, ripping in two.

I began to call out. "God help me! Please help me! Oh God! Help me!" I threw my weight onto Michael and then back toward the midwife. The driver watched, his pupils not unlike Michael's, dilated to the size of dimes. The midwife, who'd been looking out the window, instructed the driver to pull up near the emergency room entrance. Michael dashed out of the car to get a wheelchair. "God help me! Please help me!" The midwife turned her head, her hair trailing streaks of neon.

"God is helping you," she said.

Even as she said it, I knew it was true, and it continued to be as I lay on the birthing table and my daughter emerged through me like a lit match makes a hole in paper.

After Michael left and Abbie was taken to the nursery, I slept fitfully, awakened every hour by the rain and wind beating at the hospital window. The nurse wheeled the Plexiglas cradle into my darkened room after midnight and told me I needed to hold the baby, as she'd been crying in the nursery. I was exhausted and wanted to sleep. Couldn't the baby just stay in the nursery till the sun came up? The nurse insisted, laying the baby on my chest. Her weight was exquisite, like warm flour in a satin pillow, her tiny features snuffling against my collarbone until she finally fell asleep.

At home we got into a routine. Michael went to bed around eleven. I stayed up with the baby, walking from window to window with her high on my shoulder. She howled like a tiny woodland creature. In the medicine-cabinet mirror my face was fragmented; a bit of chin, eyelashes. My life had been dismantled and I could rebuild it only furtively. Motherhood was different than I'd anticipated; I thought the baby would be vulnerable and I'd be the strong and competent one. But things were reversed. I was fragile and weepy and the baby was sinewy, strong. She had no problem letting me know exactly what she wanted. Hunger enraged her. Her face turned red, then purple, then finally pink-white before she latched onto my nipple and sucked.

I watched snow fall through the cone of streetlight. Just as I learned the difference between my daughter's cries—the hungry cry, the wet-diaper cry, the bored cry, the it's-been-five-minutes-I-need-some-attention cry—I also learned the sounds different species of snow make against the glass. Tiny flakes sounded like sugar granules hitting the pane, the bigger wet flakes like sloshy rain. I learned that the radiators turn on exactly every four hours and thirteen minutes, not randomly as I'd thought before, and that my right-side neighbors took a shower each night at 12:25. I recognized all my neighbors' telephones: the mechanical bird sound, the old-fashioned ring. I heard the cats on the left playing in the night and could even distinguish the sound of their paws; Ethel scurried while Caroline was languid. I could tell how, when my husband dreamed, his breath became shallow and he shifted his legs against the sheets. I heard the two clocks, the droning electric in the kitchen, its second hand moving around the numbers, and the soft, kittenish tick of the one in the living room.

Every morning at ten when the Jamaican babysitter arrived, I ran down Hicks Street to my brother David's apartment in Cobble Hill and wrote at his kitchen table. I drank glass after glass of water so I'd be ready to breast-feed as soon as I got home. When my baby was born, I was two-thirds of the way through my novel *Jesus Saves*. The novel had two main characters: Ginger, a suburban minister's daughter, and Sandy, a thirteen-year-old girl who's been kidnapped and is being methodically tortured by her troll-like captor.

I was worried before I had the baby that once I was a mother I'd be unable to connect with the gothic tone of the book. But the opposite was true. Though I had just given birth, it was death I was obsessed with. At any time of day, without warning, my mind seized on images of my daughter in terrible, bloody disarray. I found myself grateful for the novel's dreamy sequences of surreal violence. Sandy is kept tied up under a bed and I myself, when the baby was sleeping and my husband out, squirmed under my bed and lay out under the box spring with my arms spread to the bed frame. I spent a lot of time in this position.

Initially Michael and I had been united in our common belief that life was sad. Michael dealt with this melancholy by playing his records, drinking beers, wisecracking. Nobody was more fun at a party. At first I'd been enthralled by this strategy. In the early months of our relationship, Michael and I sometimes spent whole weekends in bed. Other times we'd stay up dancing till dawn. But after having the baby I realized I couldn't outrun my longing and my loneliness.

One of our worst arguments happened one morning after he'd stayed out late. I heard his key in the lock at seven o'clock in the morning. He went right into Abbie's room, picked her up out of her crib, and put her into her high chair in the kitchen. Wearing my flannel nightgown I walked into the kitchen and asked where he'd been. At first he insisted he'd been home for a while, but I told him I'd just heard him come in.

"I was out with friends," he said. "I didn't call because I didn't want to wake the baby."

I started to cry and I saw how Michael's body straightened and his face turned red. "Why are you always making such a big deal out of things? I didn't do anything."

This was his usual line. As long as he wasn't actually sleeping with somebody else, he didn't see why I should be upset. As he saw it, staying out all night, ogling young girls, all the other behaviors that discombobulated me, were just his attempt to have fun. My emotions made Michael angry; he saw them solely as restricting his behavior, as censorious. That morning I found myself, as I had so many times before, trying to convince him that he'd hurt me. He just got stiffer and more accusatory. He said again that I made a big deal out of everything. His pupils dilated and he retreated, sitting on the kitchen stool, his eyes filling with water. He wouldn't answer any of my questions. He just stared at Abbie, who was picking up Cheerios one by one and putting them into her mouth.

Ever since I'd been a child I'd assumed I would be happy once I had a husband and a baby, but now that the struggle to acquire these things was complete, I could see the vast spiritual wilderness at the center of my life. I needed to find a way to live within this bewilderment rather than pretend that everything was all right. I began to go to noon mass at the Catholic church on Garden Place. I was at the very center of life, but it was lonely there. Giving birth had been traumatic and spectacular, had left me with a hint of life's grandeur—its meaning and texture—but it felt as if there was no place for this feeling to unfurl or manifest itself.

Abbie was mesmerized by the alcove at the church that held the Holy Mother, votive candles flicking on Mary's bare ceramic feet. The white-haired minister recited the noonday liturgy like a man back from the dead. I sat in the pew and let the words drone over me. I had in desperation begun to pray, not in any specific place—I could be nursing the baby, or vacuuming, and all of a sudden I'd feel as if my heart were pierced by a cold nail and I'd pray *Help me* with incoherent desperation.

CHAPTER 18

I N 1999 I WAS awarded the Grisham Fellowship at the University of Mississippi. Abbie and I moved for the year to Oxford, Mississippi. Michael visited once a month. My bedroom had fleur-de-lis wallpaper and a peach silk Victorian couch. The windows were covered by wood shutters. At night the room was completely dark, a darkness impossible in Brooklyn. It was too quiet, a quiet interrupted only by the sound of the neighbor's wind chimes. The house was the most elegant place I'd ever lived. It was gently worn. Paint chips blew off the front porch and the gutters, filled with leaves, sagged.

In the late afternoon, while Abbie napped, I sat on the lawn under a water oak. The light was low and transfiguring. The leaves were backlit, everything moved, and the world was a beautiful place. Once Abbie was up from her nap we'd walk across to Faulkner's dilapidated mansion. At twilight the big white house had a patina like the inside of a shell and Abbie chased fireflies among the cypress trees and boxwood hedges. The place was full of odd details that evoked Faulkner: the plastic shoe rack in an upstairs bedroom, names and numbers written on the wall in pencil by the rotary phone in the kitchen, the painting of a mule resting on the mantel in his office. The proprietor of the house told me that when Faulkner's first child was born prematurely, he and his brother had driven to Memphis in search of an incubator. I heard, too, that while everyone else was in church Sunday mornings, Faulkner rode his horse around the town square. His favorite drink was a black velvet, half champagne and half Guinness stout.

When it got dark, bunnies hopped out of the boxwoods and Abbie would chase them. As we walked over the white gravel path back toward our house, it was so dark I could barely see Abbie walking behind me. I'd focus on her quick movements, but whenever she paused she'd dissolve into the darkened landscape. Fireflies crossed in the air, floating along like loose embers.

Our closest neighbors were Dr. and Mrs. Howorth, Oxford's most elegant couple. Both had white hair and old-style manners. Whenever we appeared at their pool around five, Dr. Howorth came out holding a Popsicle for Abbie and a gin and tonic for me. Abbie, who was three, sometimes ran around naked on their huge expanse of grass and once asked me, near the end of our stay, if she could "poop in their yard for a treat." Abbie loved the magnolia blossoms, each velvet petal bigger than her hand. At Mother Goose Daycare, where she spent mornings while I wrote, she played with the plastic beauty parlor set and drove the Big Wheels around the asphalt lot during recess. These toys were different from the wooden variety she'd acquired in Brooklyn. Abbie talked about Miss Polly, the school's cook, and told me the food I made was icky compared to Miss Polly's fried catfish and rice and beans.

I had been passing through some years of fret and strife, beauty and ugliness, even some weeks of sadness and despair. There had been periods of intense joy but seldom had there been the quiet beauty and happiness I had now. I had thought all those years that I had freedom, but now I felt that I had never known real freedom nor even had knowledge of what freedom meant.

I strolled Abbie around the streets with the grand houses. A blue-haired lady sat with a blanket on her lap, attended by an African American aide in a white uniform and nurse's shoes. One Sunday I saw a family sitting around a long table in a formal dining room with a chandelier and magnolia wallpaper. In the evenings, after I put Abbie to bed, I'd read in the glow of my bedside lamp. After hours of reading, I'd feel my loneliness hovering like an aura around me, though after a month or two I realized that my loneliness, an empty and wretched vessel, was filling up as though wine were being poured into a crude and rudimentary cup. This *wine* was a mysterious substance. Its existence gave me the first sense that I might be, at intervals at least, let out from under my own gloomy and limited point of view. I'd look up from my book, lamplight spilling over my bedspread and the library books spread over my night table, and I'd say, *Why are you here?*

No answer came back, so I'd lie there listening to the sound of the wind chimes and watching the green wallpaper, its pattern improved and complicated by the shadows from the window, where vines pressed up to the glass.

In Oxford, for the first time in my adult life, I was master of my own stereo. In Brooklyn Michael had control of our music but in Mississippi I bought the local label Fat Possum's CDs, earthy music by R.L. Burnside and Junior Kimbrough. I grew fond of Fred McDowell and Memphis Minnie and I even bought an Elvis CD. There was something in Elvis's voice, a lush sense of sadness and self-acceptance, that drew me, a few months after I arrived, to Graceland.

As I waited for the tour to begin I browsed the gift shop across from Graceland. Elvis's image was printed on everything from baby rattles to underwear. I'd been warned that Graceland's interior was unbelievably tacky. I was already somewhat familiar with the white couches and jungle-room fountain. In Roanoke there is a miniature Graceland. As teenagers, my girlfriends and I would drive over to Riverdale Road and walk the little path through Don and Kim Epperly's yard to the dollhouse-sized Graceland in back. Kim, a local hairdresser, and her husband built all the tiny furniture and had replicated the carpets and wallpaper, even down to the embroidery on the bathroom's tiny towels.

So when I entered the full-sized Graceland, the magnified effect of objects I'd seen small was magical. In Graceland light seems to come at you from all directions, as if the sun has liquefied and flowed into the floor, walls, and ceiling. I recognized in the glittery decor a longing for transcendence that is often labeled as tacky. The mirrored bar in the downstairs TV room was like a fenestral opening, the kind I spent most of my childhood searching for. I also liked the modest colonial kitchen. I could easily picture a bummed-out and overweight Elvis, wondering what life was all about as he raided the refrigerator.

In the subtly lit annex where Elvis's memorabilia is held, I walked past his gold lamé suit and striped *Jailhouse Rock* shirt. The famous white bodysuit moved me most, though: the embroidered red, white, and blue eagle, the cape, the rhinestone superhero belt all held me in their messianic glow. I'm not a particularly patriotic person—if the Japanese bought the Liberty Bell I wouldn't care much—but Elvis's bodysuit was different; I had a visceral feeling that Elvis's costumes must stay in the United States of America. They were the most completely American objects I had ever seen. They radiated glamour, sadness, faith.

I wandered around the darkened corridor of the annex. I realized that Elvis was an icon, but not in any contemporary sense. He wasn't an icon in the sense that Martha Stewart is one, someone who represents a kind of lifestyle. Elvis was an icon in the traditional sense of icons of the Greek Orthodox Church. These icons depict Christ, Mary, or a saint against a gold background that signifies a source of light independent of them. In iconography gold paint is built up from the base and the figure emerges from this globe of illumination. The gold light signifies the holy other, a higher power. God. For the first time I understood Elvis's iconic status: that what he looked like or represented was less important than the fact that many people accepted that Elvis was divine.

Thunderstorms in Mississippi were violent. Rain lashed the side of the house, beat against the windows. Abbie cried out from her crib and I'd get her and let her sleep beside me. In her fluffy one-piece pajamas she was restless, pressing into me urgently like a puppy against a mother dog. I'd listen to the branches whoosh around in the wind and the zillion drops of water falling on the roof. I'd think about Michael's flat stomach, his sharp hips, his quick smile, and his enthusiasm for thrift-store finds. But I also thought about how I couldn't communicate with him. I felt like a rabbit trying to talk to a fish. I could not decide what to do. The idea of breaking up my family was horrific to me. So I'd lie listening to the house creaking and the rain spattering against the window. I knew something was happening. I read *The Cloud of Unknowing*, a twelfth-century rumination on the nature of God and being, written by some unknown mystic. I tried to follow its advice— to look, during prayer, over the shoulder of unwanted thoughts, or to huddle down under them like a coward pretending to be dead during a battle. But the teaching that gave me the most relief dealt with God's aloofness: "As long as a man lives in this mortal flesh, he will always see and feel this thick Cloud of Unknowing between himself and God."

It was a comfort to know that God didn't have to come with blazing eyeballs for me to believe in something bigger than the world I knew. My cloud of unknowing was made of purple smoke, the haze I had seen at a Prince concert. I'd imagine myself dressed in a moss-green handkerchief skirt and satin bodice. I fantasized that I was a wood nymph, lying on a velvet bed trying to commune with God.

In April I drove to Jackson to speak at a prep school literary festival. On the way I listened to a recording of Thomas Merton lecturing on Faulkner. I'd checked the tape out of the library because I felt close to Faulkner. The lecture was recorded in 1965 at Gethsemani, where Merton was novice master. Merton's Long Island accent and self-deprecating humor disarmed me. He said that the absolute worst thing a person could do was to make himself a "spiritual person." This was, according to him, completely useless. "The one thing for anyone to become, the only valuable thing, is to become yourself." This, he warned, would take a great deal of work.

Merton talked about Faulkner's story "The Bear." In it a boy, a young veteran of many hunting trips, begins to notice how different the woods sound when a bear is near. The sound of the wind, the crunching leaves, the woodpecker are all the same. But the bear's proximity, his mysterious presence, resonates in the familiar sounds. The boy realizes that though he hasn't seen the bear, the bear has seen him. "This," Merton said, "is where the mystical life begins. When what you are hunting knows you are there, he knows you're around."

When I got home Abbie was already in bed. I paid the sitter and sat outside on my lawn chair. The sky was full of stars, like salt spilled on black paper. I saw one fall, a quick arc of light disappearing over the horizon. I listened to teenagers swimming in a pool down the street. Laughter. Phrases I couldn't make out, and the flat sound of splashing water. I felt weirdly deracinated, but it was not a creepy feeling. My daughter and I were not, as I had so often feared, doomed characters in the opening sequence of a horror movie. I felt we were living in the eternal moment, residing inside infinity. I raised my hand up and held it before me as a sign.

CHAPTER 19

M Y CONNECTION TO THE spiritual realm was based on little more than desperation and a little religious reading. When I moved back to Brooklyn in July, everything fell apart. I wasn't able to pray as I had in Oxford. And while I sometimes felt a presence in the apartment, it was more sinister than peaceful. I should have gone to church with my dad, or sought a spiritual director. Instead I fell back into bad habits.

Michael, worried about my adjustment, had fixed up the apartment for our arrival, putting tile down in the bathroom and patching cracks in the ceiling. While he still fixated on young girls, talking endlessly about Britney Spears and the interns in his office, there was something new in his demeanor, a forced cheerfulness that made him seem slightly hysterical. His shoulders were always stiff and his collarbone tense and protruding. Our relationship had lost all its natural rhythm and was now like a badly timed high school play.

Abbie relished being back in the apartment and seeing her father every day. She had curly blonde hair and her baby belly protruded, pushing up her T-shirt. She was talkative and loved to tell jokes, sometimes ones she made up herself. Question: Why did the seed become a flower? Answer: Because it was bored. Sometimes she gave her jokes gothic twists. Question: Why did the umbrella bleed? Answer: Because the chicken crossed the road.

After I got Abbie to bed, I sat with Michael on the couch. He was boyish and adorable as he told me, after several beers, about a girl we both knew whom I'd babysat when I was in college. She was a teenager now. Through me Michael had met her the summer before and they'd been e-mailing. Michael told me, with a sort of reverence in his voice, that the girl had been confiding in him about her boyfriend. They were getting serious and Michael was trying to get the details. I felt tendrils of anger grow out of my heart as I looked at his face. Michael believed that getting close to young girls and hearing about their love life was so exciting that anyone, even his own wife, would understand the Masonic pull. I asked him again if he'd consider going with me to marriage counseling.

Michael grinned widely as he always did when I made the suggestion.

"No way," he said. "There's nothing wrong with me. You're the one that's changed."

"Just a few sessions?"

"You want to know why I won't go? You really want to know?"

I nodded.

He stood up, grabbed my hand, and pulled me forcefully over the carpet, past the lamps with the bronze angels. I assumed he was leading me to bed. That he wanted to communicate with me the only way that was still possible. But he passed by the bedroom door. He held my hand loosely as he had when we first got together and we'd walked around the East Village. He led me to the full-length mirror on the closet door, flipped on the overhead light, and, with a hand on each of my shoulders, pointed me at the glass. In the mirror I saw my jeans and the oversized wool sweater that had belonged to my dad. I was barefoot and my toes were chalky, the nails pale purple. My greasy hair was held in a ponytail. Michael had complained before that he wanted to see me in miniskirts, my hair down, with a little mascara, like before I had the baby. Was this what he meant as he stared over my shoulder into the glass? He smiled slightly, a strange sheepish grin, and didn't say anything. I was just as thin as before I had Abbie but my breasts had sagged a little. During one of our fights he told me that if I was eighteen, we'd never fight because he'd worship me completely. I knew he found the realities of my body tiresome and unappealing. But I think in that moment, which felt as honest to me as any I'd ever had with him, he was showing me how he saw me. He was showing me myself as he saw me now, without divinity, and even I could see that without God I was just a meat puppet, a material object no different from a chair or a couch.

After I moved into my new apartment in Fort Greene, my brothers brought over a pizza and we ate it on paper towels, beers balanced on boxes. Abbie, who'd initially seemed excited to be in the new apartment and to see the toys I'd bought her—a wooden U.S.A. puzzle and a set of plastic princesses—had begun to see she'd been scammed. Every time one of her uncles called to her, she said she was busy "working" in her room, setting up her little plastic figurines, as she'd always done, like altarpieces. She loved to surround her Elmo with paper strips shaped into birds' nests, or to arrange her Kelly dolls, the youngest member of the Barbie family, in a star configuration, each with a bead balanced on her forehead. Sometimes she'd find stuff at the park—a metal hinge, a blue rubber band, an old cassette tape—and she'd mix these items with the troll dolls her father bought her at the thrift store. I knew she wouldn't come out, at least partly because she felt out of sync with the lively atmosphere in the front room.

After everyone left, Abbie ate a slice of pizza while sitting on the edge of the bed. Afterward I bathed her in the bathtub. Her body was small but substantial, her skin like a giant rhododendron petal. Afterward we lay on my bed, she in her fleece sleeper and me beside her. She pointed out the star at the top of the window and wanted to sing "Twinkle, Twinkle." She told me a joke. Question: Why did the mud get on the other mud? Answer: Because it was lonely. After that she put her pacifier in her mouth and sucked softly. The sucks grew further apart and I thought she was falling asleep. My sense of failure was acute and melodramatic. This scene was nothing like a church service, though its elements—the bed, the star, the soft sound of Abbie's lips—seemed sacramental.

Abbie sat up. "Listen," she said, tipping her head and turning it toward the window.

All I could hear was the sound of traffic wheezing by on the elevated highway down the block.

"Shush!" she said, silencing my attempt to tell her about the proximity of the highway. "I think this new place is near the sea."

During the first weeks in the new apartment, a change came over me. My shoulders were no longer always up to my ears. My neck no longer cricked. My sleep, at that time, after so much nervous insomnia, had a straightforward restorative quality, like lying in warm, solidifying milk. I dreamt that a doctor told me he'd discovered my head had an extra chamber, that money appeared mysteriously in my checking account, that I could communicate with a spatula and a parking meter. Several vague but adversarial ideas fit perfectly in *one*. *The one.* The sensation of this transformation was physical—the five goes into the one—rather than intellectual. As autumn unfolded, I became entranced with a tree outside my office window on the Sarah Lawrence campus where I was teaching. The tree had brilliant yellow leaves and I was convinced this tree and I were in love with each other.

Just after I left my marriage I took up with a poet who lived in Berkeley. Even before he moved across the country we began to fight. I wasn't ready to unify with another man and I was beginning to realize that while brilliant and kind, the poet was also dangerously opinionated. He didn't believe in linear narrative structure and he questioned any observation I made, pointing out, as a committed postmodernist, that my idea was either derivative or culturally constructed. In the last weeks of our relationship I spent a lot of time defending my religious beliefs to him, even though I felt more disconnected from God than ever. The presence I felt in Mississippi had disappeared. God did begin to seem, as the poet insisted, like the Wizard of Oz, a culturally created conception sprung out of man's insecurity.

One Sunday morning, not long after the poet and I broke up, I sat in my brother David's yard behind his apartment in Park Slope and watched my father cry. Dad told us that Anne had left him, and that he suspected she was having an affair with her boss, the bishop. At sixty-five, with his blond hair, my dad usually resonated youthful energy, but now his face was a mass of wrinkles and black circles underlined his red-rimmed eyes. He kept covering his face with his hands, saying, "Anne is the love of my life." My brother's features were flat and stoic as my dad called himself an emotional moron and a loser. As he spoke, aggrandizing Anne and castigating himself, I felt the last shred of my stability decomposing like a tissue sunk into liquid.

God flew out of the world. The shower water hurt my skin and even the apartment's familiar objects—the kitchen sink, my night table—hurt me with their angular edges and material resoluteness. My own body was like an inanimate object, my feet in black high-tops were somebody else's, and my chest felt packed with sawdust. I thought a lot about the poet, his hands, his voice, his gigantic tennis shoes. How we'd tortured each other. I worried constantly about money, estimating my rent and utility bills and then adding up the money from teaching and freelance magazine work.

My daughter was grieving. This manifested itself mostly in tantrums. Once, during this time, I told her we were going to have frozen pizza and carrot sticks for dinner. She threw herself violently onto the ground and said she didn't want frozen pizza. She screamed until her face was red and snot ran out of her nose. I went into my bedroom and shut the door. After a while I heard her footsteps in the hallway.

"Why would you make me eat cold pizza?" she asked.

Another time I gave her a dollar. She was wearing overalls and she carefully folded the dollar up into a small square and stuck it first into the tiny pocket sewn to the bigger pocket on the front flap of her overalls, then into the bigger pocket, and then into each of the side pockets. I could tell a tantrum was coming on by the way she repeated her actions over and over and then began to whine that there was no place for her dollar.

I took the dollar and showed her how it fit into each of the pockets. This enraged her, and she flung herself onto the floor and flailed around. *There is no place for my dollar. No place for my dollar. No place.* I dragged her to her bedroom and sat with her until she finally fell asleep.

A week later I stood in an uptown pharmacy. I wore an oversized sweatshirt and a pair of jeans that hung off my ass. My eyes, as I tried on the sunglasses arranged on the plastic carousel, were sunk into my head. At ninety-five pounds, I was as thin as I'd ever been. I darted my eyes to the pharmacist who was filling up my prescription. She was a stout, gray-haired lady in a white lab coat, reading glasses hanging around her neck. She watched me as if I might shoplift. I'd come to the drugstore directly from Dr. Rapp's office. Dr. Rapp, my psychiatrist, had urged me to increase my Zoloft dosage and to take the pills regularly. He'd listed tranquilizers and sleeping pills with their side effects and told me that if my mind was sticking on negative thoughts, I should move it onto something more positive.

I had slept maybe ten hours in the last week and hadn't been able to keep down much food. I'd begun to feel my little apartment in Fort Greene, so near the BQE, was on the edge of the world. On the nights I didn't have Abbie I stayed at my dad's in Carroll Gardens. I tried to engage him in talks about God, the possibility of experiencing God not just now and then but all of the time. He'd shake his head as if I were crazy and tell me the plot of the mystery novel he was reading. My heart beat so fast it felt as if it would work its way out of my chest and fall like a lump of Jell-O onto the sidewalk. I paid for my drugs and stood outside the pharmacy, ripped open the prescription bag, unscrewed the childproof cap, and held the small pink pill between my fingers.

CHAPTER 20

I CRAWLED ONTO A wobbly pharmaceutical shelf. I could still see the hole roiling beneath me and knew my position was tenuous. I saw my therapist weekly, and while I was no longer achey and nauseous *all the time*—I could eat a little and get out of bed, I could stroll my daughter through the park and push her on the swing—I still felt fragile. The antidepressants were necessary now, but I knew drugs would neither bring back my mental health permanently nor lead to any sort of lasting transformation.

Medicated or not, I was steeped in sin.

It's old-fashioned to talk about sin, nutty and extreme, like a tent preacher damning the local prostitutes. Many of the things the Bible defines as sin—gay sex, sex before marriage, men approaching the altar with one arm shorter than the other—are clearly not sins. Meanwhile sin in the popular imagination connotes a terrible act like rape or murder. The sort of sin I am talking about consists of mundane, daily acts that separated me from my own goodness and therefore from God. I was oppositional, *going against others' ideas simply to* maintain power. I had trouble keeping secrets. I was often imperious and superior. I wasn't comfortable with my own ambivalence and so would overestimate my affections. I was often overly enthusiastic, a quality I share with my father, and one that wears away reality. I judged everything from people's shoes to the books they read. I was hardest on myself. I'd see my face in the mirror and despise the little lines around my eyes. I thought I sounded giddy and sophomoric while talking to my editor. My prose was banal and simplistic.

I knew Thomas Merton believed that God gave man a nature that was ordered to the supernatural life: "He created man with a soul that was made not to bring itself to perfection in its own order, but to be perfected by him in an order infinitely beyond the reach of human powers." God was calling my name in restaurant bathrooms, on the Q train, from the water that streamed from the showerhead, and on the sidewalk along Flatbush Avenue.

In Mississippi, I tried to contact God myself. Now I knew I needed some help. I thought about the elderly priest at the church in Brooklyn Heights. I'd gone to his rectory once and waited outside his office while he talked on the phone. Anne, my former stepmother, was an even more likely choice, but her rejection of my father made it impossible for me to talk to her about faith. Sensing this, Anne suggested I seek spiritual direction from the Community of the Holy Spirit, an Episcopal convent up at 113th Street near Columbia.

On my first visit to the Community of the Holy Spirit I was late. The subway poked through the tunnel and by accident I got off a stop too early. It was raining so hard my umbrella kept blowing backward. Anne had told me that the Holy

Spirit nuns were liberal, but I couldn't shake the image of the archetypal mean nun. Built like a battle-ax, she would rap my knuckles with a ruler and make me kneel on the cold floor and say a million Hail Marys. A friend told me how a nun, her junior high teacher, had shown her a lily. "This is you," she told my friend just before throwing the lily to the ground and crushing it with her black orthopedic shoe. When she retrieved the flower, the petals were crushed and greasy looking. "And this will be you if you have sex before marriage."

A petite woman with hazel eyes and wire-rimmed glasses opened the door. "I'm Leslie," she said. "I was getting worried about you."

I apologized for being late as I followed her into the convent. On the wall hung black-and-white photographs of older nuns, Mother Ruth and Sister Mary Christabel. The reception room had a green velvet couch and patterned carpet, on the mantel was a figurine of Mary holding baby Jesus, and in a glass case were relics of the order's early members: an old watch, a gold locket, crucifixes.

Sister Leslie was diminutive under her black robe. Her small face jutted out of her wimple. She wore a wooden cross with a silver inlay of the seven-point star. I talked fast, running through my divorce, my stepmother leaving my father, my depression, my shaky state of mystification. I finished embarrassed and nearly out of breath. My cheeks burned and I knew my clavicle was getting spotty, as it always does when I feel humiliated.

"At the moment," I said, "I am kind of a mess."

Sister Leslie, her hands resting palms up, fingers curled between one another like a pink flesh flower, smiled.

"You were being smoothed," she said. "Now God is calling you to her."

Her. The *her* made a tiny bomb go off inside my heart. She began in diagnostic mode, asking me questions about my religious life.

"Do you pray?"

"I tried when I was living in Mississippi," I said, "but I don't now."

"Do you go to church?"

"Sometimes. But I'm ambivalent about it."

"You're very hard on yourself."

"Oh, yeah," I said.

Sister Leslie sat forward. I could almost see her brain working in her forehead.

"First off," she said, "I'd like to get you praying every day. Are you familiar with centering prayer?"

I shook my head.

"It's much like meditation. You sit in a quiet place, reposed, repeating a simple word or phrase. As ideas come to your mind, images, thoughts, you let them flow past you and return to the word or your breath. Try it for ten minutes a day."

Centering prayer, I would learn, is an effort to jab a stick in the spokes of thinking, to calm what the Hindus call the monkey mind. One writer, Cynthia Bourgeault, explains the technique this way: "Pretend you are a scuba diver, sitting on a rock, watching the bottoms of boats (thoughts) move by, you see them through your mask, but rather than attach to them, you let each flow by one after another, while remaining on your rock in a deep place of peace."

"What about going to church?" I asked. One of the things I'd been dreading about this session was that Sister Leslie would insist I attend services.

"Why go," she said, "if it's just because you think you should?"

I wanted to jump into Sister Leslie's lap and have her tell me that God, that beautiful girl in the sky, loved me. She seemed so sure. Peace and faith radiated off her. Sister Leslie pulled a matchbook from the folds of her habit, her gesture like a magician making a coin appear between thumb and forefinger. She struck the match and lit the wick of the little votive candle residing on the side table.

"Before you go," she said, "let us pray."

I can't remember exactly what she said. I felt like I was in a scene from *The Sound of Music*. There was a sense of unreality in being with a nun. During my first months in Ireland, I assumed the monks I saw on the street in brown robes, rope belts, and sandals were extras for TV commercials.

I do remember the end of the prayer, something about thanking God for the confusion that had brought me here. When the prayer was done, she handed me two xeroxed short stories, one by Tolstoy and one by Edna O'Brien, and told me she'd see me at the same time the following week.

After I put my daughter to bed that night I read Tolstoy's story "A Vision at Sea." An archbishop traveling by boat from Archange to Solovki visits three holy hermits who live on a deserted island. He finds that while ancient, they are illiterate and ignorant of church doctrine. The archbishop spends all day teaching them the Lord's Prayer. Late in the evening, back on the moving ship, the archbishop sits on deck, under the stars, feeling pleased and congratulating himself for helping the simple old men. Then he sees a globe of golden light. As the light approaches the ship, he sees the three old men, toothless in their loincloths and antiquated cassocks, running over the sea as if it were dry ground. They run up next to the boat and address the bishop.

"O servant of God . . . we have forgotten it all—it is all gone from us. None of it can we recall. Teach us thou it again."

The archbishop crosses himself, bends over the bulwark to the old men, and says: "Your prayer too, O ancient men of God, was profitable unto the Lord. It is not for me to teach you. Pray you rather for us sinners."

I'd always known instinctively that doctrine was less important than an individual's personal connection to God. Now I saw that Sister Leslie agreed and lived by this idea. She was one radical nun, exclusively concerned with the movement of the spirit. I was ecstatic. For years I had felt the church and everything that came with it—rigid church ladies, dogmatic prayers, theologically simplistic sermons—had been blocking my communion with divinity. I wanted God but I couldn't see how I'd ever reach her if I had to drag along all that dead weight.

My father, since I moved out of the rectory in Williamsburg, never pressed me to go to church. I knew he thought I had an immature attitude toward communal worship. I couldn't fake it. I didn't like going to church. I didn't want to feel that the only way to God was through the Lord's Prayer. After reading Tolstoy's story, I prepared for bed by reviving my old prayer practice, one of the techniques I'd learned from *The Cloud of Unknowing*. I pretended I was resting in the huge cupped palm of God's hand. Sort of like Fay Wray sleeping against the fleshy part of King Kong's thumb, it was a peaceful sensation. There was no order of service, no hymnal, no ladies staring at my tattoo, no balding dude in the pulpit, just my cheek against the body of my creator.

* * *

My second reading assignment, Edna O'Brien's "Christmas Roses," had a different confounding effect on me. Miss Hawkins, the story's main character, is a former dancer and professional mistress who at fifty-five now takes care of a municipal garden in London. She's an eccentric older lady who lives in a one-room flat with her little dog, Clara. She dyes her hair red and sometimes puts on her black costume and stiff-necked white blouse and rouges her cheeks. She loves her garden and cares for it assiduously, picking stray leaves out of the flower beds and patting dirt down around the crocuses. One morning, looking out her window, she sees a blue tent. Sleeping inside the tent is a boy of twenty with soft brown hair, white, angelic skin, and thick, sensual lips. When she wakes him the boy is apologetic and friendly, but Miss Hawkins asks him to leave. He doesn't, and he begins helping with her gardening. She teaches him the Latin names for the flowers, invites him for coffee. He asks her to the theater and afterward she gives him voice lessons. Miss Hawkins is aware of the danger in the beautiful boy's proximity. When he asks her to the theater, at first she insists he ask someone his own age. When she feels the urge to go into a bar with a young escort and have a drink, she slaps herself.

But affection grows between the two. The boy tells her he has to vacate the flat he's sharing. She invites him to move in with her. The boy is thrilled, but while he goes to gather his belongings, Miss Hawkins recalls the chain of losses in her former life: the lover who jilted her, the man who proposed though he was already married, her final tour in the provinces "where people laughed and guffawed at her and even threw eggs."

After hours of anguish, Miss Hawkins leaves a note on her door—"YOU MUST NEVER EVER UNDER ANY CIRCUMSTANCES

COME HERE AGAIN"—and flees on the train to the country. The story concludes: "Miss Hawkins was willing to concede that she had done a very stupid thing indeed, but that it had to be admitted that it was not the most stupid thing she could have done. The most stupid thing would have been to welcome him in.'"

I finished the story on the Q train as it passed over the Manhattan Bridge and the sky was filling with raspberry-colored clouds. I was terribly confused as the train beat back the metal gutters and plunged again into the dark tunnel. Unlike Tolstoy's story, the religious significance of O'Brien's escaped me. I felt sad for Miss Hawkins, who had missed an opportunity. But I myself was forty and divorced. I knew an older woman had to protect herself from younger men's infatuations. But I was confused why Sister Leslie wanted me to read it. Maybe she was a feminist as well as a radical Christian, and the story was meant to bolster my instinct for self-preservation.

When I arrived at the convent the next week the community had changed from black robes to smart blue summertime linens, and Sister Leslie looked lighter and more ethereal. I settled into the wing chair across from her. She asked me what I thought of the stories.

"I love the Tolstoy," I said, and proceeded to explicate all my ideas about individual spirituality versus church doctrine.

She nodded. "What about the O'Brien story?"

By the question inscribed in her features, I could tell she suspected I was confused. I didn't know what to say. Already I wanted to please her. I liked the story, it was well written, full of good details and insights.

"Clearly," I said, "that boy would have broken Miss Hawkins's heart." I paused, trying to get a read on Sister Leslie's features, which remained open and intent. "I mean, she had to protect herself, right?"

Sister Leslie leaned forward, her hands clasped before her. "That boy," she said, "was God calling Miss Hawkins into a new life, a new intimacy."

Her interpretation set off another little bomb in my heart, but this one was less about spiritual freedom and more about terror. I'd come to Sister Leslie because I was sick of my mental chaos, sick of feeling raw and vulnerable. I wanted a program that would protect me. But what Sister Leslie seemed to be saying was that faith meant coming to terms with vulnerability and ambivalence, being open to everything, no matter how unconventional. I was beginning to understand that a closer relationship with God would not protect me from pain. I would, in fact, have to do what Miss Hawkins was unable to do: make myself open to sorrow.

I'd been in therapy on and off for years. I assumed my sessions with Sister Leslie would have a similar rhythm. I told her how upset I was about breaking apart my family and how mean my husband had been to me. I complained about how unhappy my mother was. Sister Leslie nodded and looked concerned when my story became harrowing. Finally she said gently but firmly: "The ambivalent parts of your life, the painful parts, Darcey, these are the holy parts. This is where God resides."

"God resides in my misery?"

"Sorrow is a conduit. It is human misery, not pleasure, that contains the secret of divine wisdom."

Our sessions began to follow a pattern. I would explicate

some problem. Sister Leslie would let the problem breathe a little, giving it some distance from the particular way I'd bracketed it. I'd continue to insist that my problem, whatever it might have been, was overwhelming, unsolvable. I'd be adamant about keeping my problems intact. Sister Leslie would say, "Be gentle with yourself," or "What is the opportunity here?" She would ask, "Do you really want to die in this ditch?" and insist in the kindest way possible that fixed meaning is less important than living with and facing my problems. "God is working in you, trying in this problem to get your attention. The clutching to the idea, to that narrow thinking, limits everything."

Unlike my shrink, who had encouraged me to put negative thoughts out of my mind, Sister Leslie encouraged me to welcome them. Not to welcome intolerable events, but to welcome the fear of them. One does not welcome cancer but one can welcome fear. Cynthia Bourgeault explains this idea in her book *Centering Prayer and Inner Awaking*: "What you are welcoming is the physical or psychological content of the moment only, not a general blanket condoning the situation." She admits that the teaching is paradoxical. "Common sense tells you that the unruly emotion is the problem and the solution is to eliminate it. But by welcoming it instead, you create an atmosphere of inner hospitality. By embracing the thing you once defended yourself against or ran from, you are actually disarming it, removing its power to hurt you or chase you back into your smaller self."

Sister Leslie used the example of Mary Magdalene going to Jesus's tomb, carrying spices to anoint his dead body. When she sees the stone has been rolled away from the sepulchre, she is afraid, she is terrified—it's the moment in horror movies when the door in the creepy house swings wide.

"She goes inside the tomb," Sister Leslie said excitedly, the words spilling out fast and her hands fluttering. "And what she finds is nothing; she's been looking for a dead thing, but what she finds is that the tomb is *empty*."

PART FIVE

CHAPTER 21

ONE SUNDAY DURING LENT I wake with the taste of pennies in my mouth, my chest sore, the same broken record of worries running through my head. I worry about money and wonder whether Abbie, who's been struggling with her math homework, will be able to pass the third-grade test. I'm off antidepressants and having trouble controlling my anxiety. I worry about my mother, who is alone and without financial security. Panic blooms out of my chest until I am finally so sick, I pound down the stairs and grab hold of the cold porcelain toilet.

Depression is a wilderness; the landmarks of ordinary life are torn loose from their meaning. Writing in my journal, reading to my daughter, simple domestic activities: They become dry and anxious endeavors. I am in a desert like the one Jesus inhabits during Lent. In the day I can talk myself down: I have a little money in the bank. My daughter will not fall out of the window of her father's apartment. But at night I can't control my thoughts. I dream I'm talking to an Irish Catholic boy I knew in Roanoke. While we're talking, Abbie lies suspended underwater in the bathtub. Abbie gets away from my mother and runs across the interstate. My neck is tight and my sinuses ache. Lent is nearly over and I'm annoyed with Jesus. I'm frustrated he's getting so much attention. The truth is I've always felt competitive with Jesus. I resent all the holy week services, particularly because, though I'd like to attend, I can't. Abbie has homework, bedtime is at eight. I have my classes to teach, papers to grade. A friend suggests that I need to realign my priorities. This enrages me. I'm not out snorting coke and picking up sailors, I'm trying to pay my bills and make sure my daughter learns her multiplication tables. Besides, if God is equally inside me as inside Jesus, if God is equally inside a church as inside my kitchen sink, then why should I feel compelled to go to church?

"Jesus is a drama queen," I say. "Every time I see a crucifix I feel like shouting, 'Get down off that cross, you big faker!'" Sister Leslie sits across from me smiling. She sees my agitation and seems amused by it. Her face is serene, though the eyes behind her glasses sparkle. I know she won't yell at me, but I'm pretty sure she won't agree with my assessment of Jesus.

"This is a very good thing," she says, leaning forward. "You're finally feeling it. You're uncomfortable because you're up there pinned with Christ to the cross."

"Do you think God loves the rest of us as much as he loves Jesus?" I ask. It's idiotic, I know, but my soul is tightly fisted around this concern.

She leaves her chair and comes to me with a box of Kleenex, her voice low and confident. "Absolutely," she says.

Since I've been seeing Sister Leslie, the cross, which for years I'd regarded as a kitsch object for slaying vampires, has begun to resonate. I've internalized the wood slats pressed against one another and see them as a symbol of my own existential conflicts. Sister Leslie, like all of us, has had her own conflicts. She is the oldest of four children. She was eight when her twin brothers were born and ten when her sister was born. She remembers the house in chaos when all three were in diapers. "I was always longing for silence," she says. In Tonawanda, the Buffalo suburb where she grew up, she attended an American Baptist church, where she was baptized in the big tub behind the altar. After a restless decade of college, graduate school, and travel, she settled with her partner—a woman who years before had been a Catholic nun—in Manhattan, working on Wall Street as a librarian for a corporate law firm that represented Ivan Boesky. During Sister Leslie's lunch hour she sometimes sat in the back of Trinity Church and was pulled in by the beauty of the language of the Book of Common Prayer. She joined the church, got a spiritual director, and began to participate as a subdeacon and reader. Two years after her relationship broke up, she began attending day retreats at Holy Spirit. One day Sister Mary Christabel asked her a question that changed her life. "She asked me if I'd ever thought of becoming a nun. I said *no* and ran out of the place." She laughs now, thinking about her alarm. "But inside me that *no* resonated. Inside me there was a giant *yes.*"

While all the nuns were celibate, at first she assumed her homosexuality would preclude her from being accepted as a novice: "I can't be a nun, I'm gay," she said later to Sister Mary Christabel. Sister Leslie still remembers the elderly nun's response: "What does that have to do with anything?"

After 9/11 I need desperately to talk to Sister Leslie. I want to know if I have to pray for the terrorists, and what to say to friends who are condemning God. She tells me half of the order is down at the site passing out sandwiches while the other half, herself included, is spending extra time in prayer. She looks exhausted but at peace.

Her composure makes me angry. I tell her I keep thinking of flames engulfing people and the abject terror of those who jumped.

Sister Leslie is silent, her hands folded in her lap. "When one thinks of horror one must also think of ecstasy." She leans in, her thin frame balanced on the edge of the chair. "No one knows what was on the other side for those people."

I resist this idea. Downtown, a burnt-computer smell hangs in the air. The furniture in Sister Leslie's room, which usually comforts me, stands around like bad ideas. I want to provoke her. I run through my list of spiritual roadblocks. There's what happened to Michael's uncle, Ron. I'd last seen Ron at a minor-league baseball game in Illinois. I remember his red face and veiny nose, his ratty cashmere coat and worn loafers. That winter he'd come out of a bar late at night and passed out in a snowbank. By the time a passerby found him he had frostbite in his hands and legs. Both legs had to be removed, as well as all of his fingers. He was in a wheelchair, living in his mother's house, when he died of complications from the amputations.

As I lay out the grim details—the blackout, the snow, the amputations, the wheelchair—I hear my voice stopping and starting. I sound hysterical. I can tell by the way Sister Leslie is sitting that she knows I'm not just telling a story, I'm asking a question. *What is the meaning in Uncle Ron's death?* I can't make horror into anything else. I can't flow through it. I hit my head on Uncle Ron in his ratty cashmere coat lying in the snowbank, his fingers and legs turning pale purple.

Sister Leslie leans forward and speaks, her voice clear and strong.

"You'll never know the meaning of an incident like Ron's death until a much later date," she says.

This answer does not please me. It's like "time heals all wounds." I look at her. She is thin under her habit, bones covered in a black shroud.

"At some later time," she says, "the meaning, which will *never* be explicit, may reverberate."

"I don't get it."

I keep thinking she hasn't heard me. Ron had his legs sawed off. Ron had all his fingers cut off. Ron had children, sisters, brothers, a mother. The horror to me is complete. There's no room for even the smallest ray of light.

"We're here now in this room," she says. "We're talking about Ron. His story has moved you, made you aware of human frailty. Think of the horror of the crucifixion, the degradation. The shame of it." Sister Leslie leans forward. "And how that event reverberates out through history into so many hearts."

Sister Leslie is insisting that I have a choice. I can clench the bloody bone or I can widen my focus, look around me and see that while my hands may be bloodstained, I am standing in a garden under a tree surrounded by light.

CHAPTER 22

A SUNDAY MORNING. ABBIE gets up before me and sets up the chessboard. She watches cartoons while she waits. I'm always white and she's always black. Our board is made of wood and we play on our new velvet couch in our new house in the Lefferts Garden section of Brooklyn, a few blocks from Prospect Park. Our home, which I bought with my brother Jonathan, is a small wood Victorian farmhouse built in 1890. It looks like the little house in the children's book that a city grew up around. When the realtor first took me into the place, the previous owner was practicing his guitar, a composition he wrote himself entitled "Retain Some Passion."

In less than an hour, I have to take Abbie to her father's apartment in Brooklyn Heights. Her blonde hair falls over her forehead as she concentrates on her move, though while I move she gets up and does what she calls a "chess dance" beside the couch. Abbie's particularly good at maneuvering her bishop. As usual she beats me.

It's nearly ten, I tell her. Time to go. Abbie goes to her room and brings down a stuffed cat and a baby doll with a grimy face and a beige cloth body. She always brings familiar toys from my house to her father's and vice versa. Abbie is wearing her pink high-top tennis shoes, a plaid pleated skirt, and black tights speckled with multicolored stars. On the way out, she tells me she likes to have a banana for an appetizer and that her favorite time to go to bed is not eight, the bedtime at my house, but nine thirty, the bedtime at her dad's. We walk down Hawthorne, past the abandoned house with a statue of St. Francis on the front porch and several brick apartment buildings sprayed with silver graffiti. Abbie plays step on a crack break your mother's back. She is tall and sturdy for an eight-year-old, with blunt-cut blonde hair and a round, open face. Now we can step only on the "lily pads," the round bits of blackened chewing gum stuck on the sidewalk. On the B41 bus we play tic-tac-toe on a restaurant napkin I pull from my backpack. Then we look out the window and count cars. Abbie counts blue and I count red.

In Brooklyn Heights, Michael buzzes us in. He looks sleepy as he stands in the doorway in a maroon sweater. We are polite and somewhat formal during these exchanges. I find myself listing off what Abbie needs to practice: her piano, her multiplication tables. With a reserved smile Michael assures me she will. Abbie runs past her dad into her room and brings out markers and paper. She starts to draw on the coffee table. Out the window I can see it's starting to rain, so I borrow an umbrella. As I stand in the doorway, Abbie interrupts her artwork to throw her whole body against me, kissing me on the lips.

No matter how many times I drop her off at her father's, I always feel as if her life with him is her real life, and I'm just an interloper. As I ride the elevator I feel the Sunday loneliness creeping around my stomach like a greasy snake, and I know that when I get back to my empty house I'll feel painfully insubstantial. On the street, snow and rain thump against the top of my umbrella. The sidewalk is covered with slush as I climb up the steps of the B41.

My Sunday malaise has been more acute since I left my husband and created an odd bilateral family for Abbie. But the truth is I've always felt an end-of-the-week melancholy that no amount of brunch mimosas or *New York Times* Arts and Leisure sections can appease. Sunday's hours feel different to me from the other six days'. Rabbi Heschel, in his book *The Sabbath*, insists that the sixth day is a palace in time. "Things do not change on that day. There is only a difference in the dimensions of time, in the relation of the universe to God."

That's the problem: My relations with God are still mitigated. My ambivalence about church hasn't dissipated since I began seeing Sister Leslie. Still, I feel more drawn to Sunday services. If Holy Spirit was closer, I'd worship there with Sister Leslie and the other nuns. The majority of the churches in my neighborhood are of the storefront variety, but there is one large brick church near my house, Grace Reformed. I've seen ushers in gray suits pushing a lady in a wheelchair up the ramp. Once her blue hat flew off and one of the men chased the tumbling bit of color down the block. The stained glass windows, with their emberish golds and warm greens, seem mystical to me, especially when I'm walking back from the subway a little high from red wine.

The bus lets me off on Flatbush and I cross over to Lincoln. I pause in front of Grace Reformed Church, then tell myself I'll just stand a few minutes in the narthex. The interior of the church is small and old-fashioned, painted beige with a pale blue ceiling. A brass chandelier hangs before the altar. Over the arched alcove a line from Psalm 100—ENTER INTO GOD'S GATES THANKFULLY—is painted in big gold letters. Brass organ pipes line the back wall, and one stained glass window features angels with pale curly hair framed by milky glass wings.

The room is warm and an usher, a woman in a dark suit with a gold-cross lapel pin, urges me into the back pew and sticks a bulletin in my hand. West Indian American women dressed in suits and felt hats sit all around me. Reverend Banks, a stocky, handsome African American man in wire-rimmed glasses, takes the pulpit. He calls Grace "the ship of the Lord," and it does feel like a vessel with all the darkness and rain outside. Banks begins his sermon with a quote from Julian of Norwich, the fourteenth-century mystic, about her vision of Jesus and her empathetic message, "All will be well." As he preaches his face takes on a pinkish glow. He's passionate as he calls congregants "Beloved" and says, "Hello? *Somebody?*" when he hasn't gotten a response. After a while Banks comes down off the altar into the center aisle and riffs like a jazz musician, staying close to the themes and motifs of his earlier composition but letting the sound of the words run free. He entreats us not to let our positions in life, whatever they may be, keep us from serving God. He falls into rhetorical syncopation with the line "touched in the name of Jesus."

"We think we can do it all ourselves, we think we can, but we can't. We need to be touched in the name of Jesus. We have to accept that we can't be proactive, we can't do it alone, we have to let ourselves be touched in the name of Jesus. We say, 'I'm going to do it, I did it. I got closer to God, it was all me.' But we have to wait, wait in our sorrow and our grief to be touched in the name of Jesus. God does this for us. It's all God. It's none of us. God touches us in the name of Jesus."

Even from the last pew, I see Banks's forehead shiny with sweat. His glasses glint under the overhead light. I'm not used to the high emotions. In a Lutheran service the liturgy reminds us of a fantastical event that happened in the past, but here at Grace, Reverend Banks is trying to make something happen *now*. He moves from the sermon to the passing of the peace. I shake hands with a woman who tells me her name is Zena. I shake hands with an usher in a blue suit and pale pink tie, and I shake the hand of every person in the pew directly in front of me. I see a lady in the front of the church: Her hair is dyed purple and her mouth hangs in the shape of a cashew. She walks with a swing, dragging a lame leg. She hugs everyone within reach, embracing a big woman in a red suit and a tiny leopard-skin hat. I recognize in her abandon a vulnerability I've been longing for, a way of being connected to others that has little to do with mutual accomplishment. She lunges toward me. *Gawd bess ou*, she says as she hugs me. *Gawd bess ou gurl*.

Christmas eve. It's a mild night. I have on velvet pants, a leather jacket, motorcycle boots. Abbie is wearing her swingy leopard-skin dress, fake fur jacket, and black go-go boots. She wants to know why we can't stay home, drink hot cocoa, and watch *The Simpsons Christmas Special* on DVD. I explain how I went to church every Sunday as a kid, and how I miss it.

Abbie is quiet as we walk past a holly tree strung with bee lights. One yard features an inflatable Santa. A glowing paper star hangs in the window. Abbie is hopping over the cracks in the sidewalk. She says I might as well know now that she doesn't like church that much.

"I like Buddha," she says.

"Buddha is good," I agree.

"Buuudhaaa," Abbie speaks slowly, enunciating each syllable, "isssss the mmmmmmasssssster."

I nod.

"Also," she shifts gears and speed talks. "He's green, he sits
cross-legged, and he floats."

"You mean levitates?"

"Yeah, he can levitate," she says thoughtfully as we walk
through Grace Reform's black wrought iron gate and past the
evergreen strung with big old-fashioned multicolored lights.
An usher gives us bulletins and we sit in the back. The choir,
in red sweaters and brown pants, proceeds up the aisle, followed by a half dozen shepherds in brown cotton robes carrying walking sticks. The angels wear glittery wings and shifts
made from bedsheets. Joseph wears a blue velour bathrobe.
Mary wears a white lace dress with a matching turban. Once
the nativity is settled on the altar, the younger children sing
"Away in a Manager" and "What Child Is This."

Abbie is on the edge of the pew watching the children in
the nativity. She's particularly interested in Mary, who sits on
a folding chair, her hands in her lap, looking down into a
wooden manger. After Reverend Banks reads the Christmas
story, a woman passes Mary a real baby and the lights are lowered. The ushers go from pew to pew lighting candles. We
sing "Silent Night." Shadows flicker on the dark stained glass
windows and the people around me shine. "Silent Night" was
the emotional high point of the service when I was a kid. Afterward we ran home to set out milk and cookies for Santa.
But at Grace the lights come up after, and Reverend Banks
moves off the altar and begins to read from Revelations. I
look around at the people in the pews. Their faces seem less
familiar, and I realize I may not be among people who explic-
itly share my beliefs. Grace Reformed parishioners listen to

the verses of Revelations, the four horsemen, the lion with horns growing out of his head. The baby Jesus begins to whine and reach his hands out to the front pew. He strains his tiny arms.

A few weeks later Abbie has lined up her Hello Kitty dolls along the tub's edge and her Barbie Jet Ski is zipping around in the water. She's gotten two tiny glow sticks from a gumball machine and is using them like starting batons. Ever since I picked her up at school she'd been preoccupied. I ask her what is wrong. She looks up at me from the tub.

"Quintana told me something that's really going to hurt your feelings."

Quintana, a girl in Abbie's class, is a sophisticate with a Danish mother and an older Spanish father. Maybe she said something disparaging about my ratty wool sweater and baggy jeans, but who knows? Once, when she was in preschool, Abbie asked me where poop came from. I began to tell her about the digestive tract and how vitamins and nutrients are taken out of food and absorbed by the body. Abbie's eyes glazed over. "Zachary says the wolves come and put poop in you at night." She said her answer was definitive.

After I read to her she snuggles down into her bed, her two dolls Pussy Cat and Kit beside her, the glow sticks each balancing against their chests. I ask her again if she wants to tell me.

"It's going to really hurt your feelings," she says. "I hate to say it to you."

"Go ahead," I say.

"Quintana says there is only Mother Nature, there is no God."

"That doesn't hurt my feelings," I say. "That's fine with me."

"Really?" she is incredulous.

"Everybody has their own theology."

She looks at me blankly.

"You know how your friend Ginger believes in werewolves and she prays to her dog Dudley?"

Abbie nods.

"Everybody has their own idea of God. I mean maybe Quintana is right, maybe Mother Nature is God. Sister Leslie thinks God is a girl."

Abbie's mouth drops open.

"God is a girl?" she says.

"Sister Leslie thinks so," I say.

Her brows fold down and she looks, in her eight-year-old way, extremely serious.

"I need to know if God is a boy or a girl."

"You can decide," I say to her. "You decide what you want to believe."

"God is a girl?" Abbie says again as I turn off the bedside lamp. "I'll have to think about that."

In the dark, the glow sticks lie on her dolls as bright as bits of neon.

"Look, Mommy," she says. "The dolls have souls."

At first Abbie fights me every Sunday morning. Why can't we follow Buddha? He looks so much happier than Jesus. She insists on wearing her striped soccer shirt with the black number 14 and she wants to wear shorts and her soccer cleats. *God wants me to wear this.* She refuses the more conventional cotton dress and tights I set out on her bed. Of course I'm ambivalent. I had the same argument with my mother when I wanted to wear bell-bottoms and a halter to worship service. What does it really matter if you praise God in shin guards and cleats or in a mint-colored summer suit? We compromise.

She can wear her soccer shirt with a jean skirt, and her clean pair of tennis shoes.

I sit in the balcony with other mothers doling pretzels from Ziploc bags and sticking straws into juice boxes. A little boy in a three-piece suit sprawls out on the pew. I came to Grace to worship with people on an elemental level; to experience the kind of care and connection one feels with strangers at the site of an accident or in an emergency room, where pulse and heartbeat mean more than status or wealth or whatever else people use to subdivide themselves.

Many Sundays at Grace the singing, Reverence Banks's sermon, and the group prayers seem to rise up and form a passageway, a conduit to God. But when Banks talks about being born again, I feel the passageway snap shut. I'm unsure why I can support Quintana's belief in Mother Nature while I can't tolerate the idea of a fixed set of rules for redemption. Banks also talks about the importance of certainty. I've always felt alienated from people who tell me they feel surrounded by the Love of Jesus *all the time*. Worse, while Banks is away one of the deacons includes homosexuality, along with alcohol and drugs, in a prayer for addiction. How can I worship with people who denigrate my gay friends? I skip several Sundays and think about quitting.

Sister Leslie convinces me that, in my own way, I've been called to Grace Reformed. "You need to ask God," she says, "Why do you want me here? For whatever reason—and in this life you may not know. God may want you to connect with someone there. We think so linearly. But really it's the idea of the ultimate mystery, the mystery of life. You need to trust even your own uncomfortableness. Those feelings do not mean that you're not supposed to be there. You need to be working through these feelings about people who are very different. God is asking you not to discount or exclude these people, but to try and understand them."

The Sunday I come back, Reverend Banks's sermon, "Invest Your Life in God," encourages us to take risks. "Abdicate your right to yourself," he preaches. "Don't be afraid, don't just let people who do it well do it. I always say if it's worth doing, it's worth doing poorly." He tells about his conversion on 139th Street and Adam Clayton Powell Boulevard in Harlem. Then he opens his sermon to testimonials. An older lady takes the cordless mike and tells about her depression after her grandson died, how she could not get *a ground*. Then comes the altar call. A lady in a down vest and tennis shoes with the toes cut off comes up to the edge of the altar. Reverend Banks, in his purple vestment, comes down and the woman starts to scream, *Who do you say that I am?*

CHAPTER 23

P ALM SUNDAY. THE USHERS wear white suits, white
shoes, and white stockings. Reverend Banks's sermon
centers on how we must submit to God's will. "You can go to
church to get closer to God," Banks says, as if he's speaking
directly to me. "But he does it all. God does it, not you." As I
watch Reverend Banks work himself up, I realize that many
of my life's questions have to do with orientation, how one
should be angled in relation to one's own sorrow, how one
should be oriented to others. In his sermon, Banks tries to
reorient parishioners, to make them aware that God is above
them, holding them in grace. Banks comes down off the altar
into the center aisle and tells how God so longed for us that
he sent down his son.

I am sitting in the last pew near a stained glass window
decorated with sheep and an angel in a blue gown. Behind me
the ushers sit in folding chairs, shadowed by the overhanging
balcony. Banks stamps his foot and bends over as if he has a
hitch in his side; he's trying to "get a word through." He calls
the Bible his sword; he holds it toward the ceiling. He wants

the holy spirit to come, to come down into Grace. His voice is like a wizard's incantation. It's the part in the movie when the sky darkens, lightning begins to flash, and the wind whips around. A voice squawks out like a tropical bird, and then almost simultaneously I hear a thump. One of the ushers, a short woman with braided hair, has fallen forward. She is on one knee grabbing hold of a folding chair. The ushers gather around her like agitated seagulls. Suddenly her arms fly out from her sides as if she's doing a swan dive and she's pulled back through the air, where she crashes into another folding chair. Though she is a heavy woman, her body appears as light as a dried leaf as her arms fly straight out and she's pulled backward again onto the floor. Reverend Banks continues to pray, his brow shiny now and his black robes swaying. The ushers finally stabilize the woman, lift her into a chair, and press around her as she sobs.

After the service an usher passes me a palm frond. She says I look tired and I say I've been having trouble sleeping. She tells me to pray to the holy spirit.

"Ask him," she says, "to raise a circle of fire up around your bed."

One Sunday in early September a young woman follows me out of Grace and introduces herself as Aretha Jennings. She has a wide, golden-brown face and her hair is held in hundreds of small braids. In her distinct Jamaican accent she invites me to a prayer group, one that is forming to discuss Rick Warren's book *The Purpose Driven Life*.

The first meeting is held at a home on Crown Street. The walls of Maria's apartment are yellow, with green curtains and bright floral throw pillows. Maria is from St. Lucia and has been living in the States for ten years working as a nanny. Her place is decorated like a beach cottage, with prints of the ocean and a giant vase with red silk flowers. Pictures show both the red-haired children she cares for and her son, who remained in St. Lucia with his grandmother.

I'm late and I see as I come into the living room that Rick Warren, in his signature Hawaiian shirt, is already talking on the television. Aretha gives me a disapproving look as I settle myself on the couch. Warren is an unassuming man who tells self-deprecating jokes while promising that his book will improve our lives. At the end of his message, he asks that we bow our heads and pray.

It's the first time I have ever prayed with an image on a television screen. It feels a little weird. My fellow prayer-group members seem more comfortable. Edgerton and Una have their fingers crisscrossed, heads bowed reverently. Una's long ponytail cascades down the back of her blue sweater. Edgerton is the only male member of the group, a soft-spoken security guard at NYU. Sybil, an older woman, sits beside them. Elaine, Una's younger sister, works as a registered nurse at St. Francis Hospital in Manhattan. Pat, a heavyset woman with short hair, takes care of an elderly man.

After Pastor Warren concludes, Aretha turns off the video and takes over. She is one of Grace's leaders, a strong, intelligent young woman who will attend Princeton Theological Seminary in the fall. Our theme today is "What on earth am I here for?" Aretha gives an overview of the first seven chapters of *The Purpose Driven Life*.

Warren's book is the preeminent religious self-help book. Ten percent of all churches have used *The Purpose Driven Life*'s program. The book is written in a style reminiscent of a Sunday school text, with the same combination of insipidness and enthusiasm: "Almighty God yearns to be your Friend!"

Some of Warren's message is theologically worthwhile. He describes God's love for us and says that, in our own individual ways, we can each find both grace and fulfillment. I'm less comfortable with his emphasis on spiritual certitude. He tells of a professor who mailed 250 letters to scientists and scholars, asking them what they saw as the key to life. All the answers, Warren reports, were nebulous. The intellectuals had no idea what the meaning of life was. "Fortunately," Warren writes, "there is an alternative to speculation." Certitude and obedience, not striving for complex meanings, are central to his theology. Obedience "unlocks understanding" and determines whether you can make it into heaven. "God will do an audit of your life, a final exam before you enter eternity," Warren explains.

Aretha seems annoyed with Pat, who won't stay in the confines of our workbook. "Eternity," Pat says, "is a sort of longing. It's that thing that is going to pull you back. We are going to be pulled back. That's why inside of us is always a feeling of longing."

As we go around the room and describe what we think God looks like, we imagine an old man in a robe with a long beard. When it's her turn, Pat becomes animated. How God looks doesn't matter so much to her. "My mother only had one leg," she says. "I had no father and my mother prayed twenty-four-seven. God is the man who brings the food!"

We meet for another session at Una and Edgerton's apartment on Lincoln Road. Una has steamed a salmon and prepared a salad with white beans, red onion, cilantro. There's a punch bowl filled with ginger ale and orange sherbert, chunks of pineapple floating on the frothy surface. Two identical velveteen sofas face each other, a floral carpet between. Edgerton and Una are fine hosts. Edgerton offers to refill our plates. He holds up the Good Samaritan as his role model, and his gentle manner bears this out.

I learn about the members of our group best through our communal prayer. Life has not been easy for any of them. All have immigrated from the Caribbean, all have jobs that are hard. Elaine is a single mother. She often prays, "God, help me and my son. We could do better." Aretha's stepfather crashed the car again, and her mother suffers from migraines. Pat's been having heart problems and, without insurance, has to wait weeks for treatments.

Happy as I am to get to know everyone, I'm growing more and more frustrated with *The Purpose Driven Life*. Warren seems to believe our sole purpose is to become better church members, to bring brownies to bake sales and attend committee meetings. Nonbelievers are essentially amoral and should be engaged only in an effort to convert them. And there's no explanation of vocation or passion, no sense that ones's purpose might lie outside the born-again nexus. If God infuses everything, one's passion might be to teach Russian, to play the violin, to be a social worker or a civil rights leader. I, for one, am ecstatic Picasso didn't separate his career from his true meaning. He might have ended up painting church basements instead of inventing modernism. And Jane Austen understood her purpose was to write novels, not inspirational inserts for church bulletins.

After the prayer meeting is over I ride the elevator down with Pat. Her wide brown face is twisted in displeasure, and she shifts from foot to foot, her heavy breasts swaying under her shirt. "God," she speaks in a heavy Trinidadian accent. "He talks to everyone differently. Obedience is listening to God. No one knows what God says to anyone else. That other"—she says, motioning out the elevator door—"all that we've been hearing tonight is just speculation."

On our walk home she tells me about her mother in Trinidad. How she lost her leg from complications due to her stepfather's beatings. Often they did not have enough to eat. When Pat's mother died Pat came to New York, where she worked on Long Island as a live-in maid, sending her salary home to the island where she left her children in the care of a friend, a decision she still regrets: "I was not there to water the plant." She had a fourth baby, a girl. On weekends, Pat would visit her daughter at the babysitter's but could not stay there. Neither could she bring her daughter to the house where she worked. "I wanted to be with her," Pat tells me, "so we'd ride the commuter trains back and forth all night long."

The theological differences between Aretha and me begin to show. When I complain about Bible verses I consider too didactic, she replies, "God speaks when the book is open and stops when the book is closed." Between prayer groups, we argue our doctrinal points via e-mail.

"If I sound defensive, it's more annoyance at times not so much at you but at the sameness of your argument to the liberal school," she writes. "I was told that an education is a means of learning how to think for oneself, taking a synthesis of everything and living what is best for you, but instead even in grading, I have found very few professors allow any other thoughts but theirs. Everything is relative except the 'fixed fact' that everything is relative. I found liberals to be more into brainwashing than any church. If you don't support the Gay agenda, then you are uneducated and a bigot."

I suggest, as Alan Watts has said, that literal interpretation of the Bible is a form of idolatry. Aretha disagrees.

"I don't understand everything in the word. Some things are beyond my comprehension, others cause me to cry, even cringe, but when I accept it has authority, there is a sense of clarity and peace. Has a fixed understanding of scripture helped me to act? Of course. Otherwise I would stay in bed. Although there seems to be many rules, I don't feel confined or like I am missing out on anything because I believe in the absolute goodness of God, so it's just not a problem for me."

Like me, Aretha has a little notebook with thoughts and lists. Seven Qualities of a Good Husband. Six Ways I Know I'm Ready to Be with Someone. Seven Qualities Women Want. Once, as we drove her home from church, we played my daughter's favorite car game, Dream Dinner Party. Abbie's guest list included Snoop Dogg, Joan of Arc, Elmo, Elvis, and Buddha: "They will eat fried chicken and pesto and the gift bags will contain fairy wings that will actually make you fly." Aretha had only one guest, King David from the Bible. While a deejay plays the love songs from *The Lion King*, they will slow dance. Afterward they will recline on chaise longues covered with pink satin pillows while Denzel Washington brings them bright goblets of pink virgin punch.

Our final meeting is at Sybil's house in Brownsville. Her kitchen table is spread with a rum cake, stewed chicken, and fresh-cut carrots and celery with ranch dip. The walls are covered with mirrors and there is a large television and a fish tank. Pat is home with heart trouble. The video is inserted and Rick Warren flashes up on the screen. "Christians are like fertilizer," he says. "They smell in a heap, but if you spread them around they are good for the soul." Edgerton laughs tentatively. He's an elegant man at odds with Warren's showmanship. This final session is about evangelism. "The focus of this week's lesson is to help you reach out to people who are lost and outside of God's family."

Everyone tells what they are doing to introduce nonbelievers to Christ. Aretha approaches people on the subway. Una gives out pamphlets to the elderly at her nursing home. Edgerton is helpful to people. He feels that by being a Christian example, he will interest them in Christ. Elaine has invited six women to church. Aretha insists, as Rick Warren does, that one needs to be careful in dealing with non-Christians. One must be angled at them for conversion alone. After the formal part of our class we break and stand around the kitchen table, eat cake, and drink coffee with heavy cream. A discussion begins about punishing children.

"The children here are so unruly," Edgerton says.

"Back home," Maria says, "it was spare the rod, spoil the child. My mother would put my head between her legs and beat on my face."

"We were beat," Elaine adds, "with belt buckles, with shoes, with whatever was at hand."

"Yes," Sybil agrees, "you must bend the tree from the time it is young."

"I was stubborn," Aretha says, "so my mother had to beat it out of me."

"That's how I knew my father cared for me," Edgerton says. "Because he was strict and watchful and he beat me if I went the wrong way."

Pat is home from the hospital but still on bed rest. I decide to make a visit. But first I chop carrots and green beans, brown ground turkey, and make a stew that I pack into Tupperware containers. I include a package of soft tortillas and a container of juice. I pack all this into a grocery bag and Abbie and I walk over to Pat's studio apartment on Rodgers, near the fire station.

I bang on the ground-floor window. No answer. I bang again. I assume Pat's gone to the doctor. I write her name on the bag and leave it inside the doorway. On the way home I think of my friend Tim. He worked on the Nestlé boycott, on Third World Debt reduction. He spent ten years trying to unionize Vermont's dairy farmers and several more working for Lutheran World Relief. At forty-seven he had a religious experience and subsequently went to a Methodist seminary. He's fond of saying, "The revolution will happen one casserole at a time."

In a few days I boil salmon and asparagus, and cut cantaloupe and mango for a fruit salad. I pack it all up, walk around the corner to Pat's, and knock on the window. Her face appears at the glass like a fish moving up from muddy water. She wears a worn aqua nightgown and looks tired. Inside her tiny apartment, books, videos, CDs, her daughter's stuffed animals are piled on top of each other up against the walls. Pat shows me the library book she is reading and tells me that, if tickets are cheap enough, she loves to go to the theater. She tells me about the valve at the back of her heart. It's permanently clogged. She won't be able to lift the elderly man she'd been caring for, but when she gets better she hopes to work as a baby nurse. Pat's youngest daughter is a junior at Spelman. When she was in grammar school, Pat was PTA president. I tell her I want to come see her next week. Pat says she'd love to see me. "But I don't make plans," she says. "Who knows what God might want from me next week."

CHAPTER 24

A BBIE'S DYEING EGGS WITH my mom. When I press her
to come to Easter service she reminds me that she, like
her friend Quintana, has decided there is only Mother Nature. I decide not to argue. How can you argue with a girl
wearing a Supergirl nightgown and writing YO! with a wax
crayon all over several dozen hard-boiled eggs?

It's been a cold winter and a rain-soaked March. Not long
ago I became an associate at the Community of the Holy
Spirit. In the chapel, the altar covered with a white cloth, I
was asked a few questions, all of which I answered with *I do*.
Sister Leslie anointed a medallion attached to a length of
leather in holy water and placed it around my neck. While I
am still feeling close to the nuns, my church attendance has
slipped. I go to Grace about once a month now, mostly out of
duty. Worse, I've been cheating on Grace, going some Sundays to the Catholic church on Nostrand. I already have a little crush on the priest, who talks about how the mirror is
darkened now, but how after death, the mirror will be filled
with light.

Grace and I are at that awkward stage similar to the inevitable point in romantic relationships. All the weird things have come out, the preconceptions, the unbridgeable misunderstandings. Now it's time to see if, despite our problems, we can remain together. Sister Leslie encourages me to pray. What do they mean when they say obedience? What do they mean by certainty? She points out that my defenses are up. My resistance to certain ideas are things God wants me to confront. She advises that I pray into the static.

Inside Grace the altar is covered with potted lilies, pink tulips, and daffodils. The place is humid and sweet as a greenhouse. Ushers wear white skirts with yellow blouses. As the choir processes, the congregation sings, "I Know That My Redeemer Lives." We hold hands across the rows for the peace song. Reverend Banks begins his sermon by explaining how Easter originated as a pagan holiday named after the goddess Oestar, and that Persians dyed eggs long before Christ was born. Banks goes on to describe the crucifixion, the thorns puncturing the skin of Jesus's forehead, blood streaming down his chin, how he passed the dark night in the tomb and then how his resurrected body filled with nothing but light.

I am lucky if I can believe in the resurrection ten minutes a month. I have doubt. But I have faith as well. My doubt fuels my faith. To me doubt connects to the mystery of God much more than certainty. The finite cannot contain the infinite. Once, a New York cab driver told me he was a former Muslim who now subscribes to no organized religion. He said he was reading Anne Lamott's writing guide, *Bird by Bird*, to help him write a book that lays out his theological ideas.

"Religions are not directly from God," he said animatedly from the front seat. "Religion is finite. God is not finite, but infinite."

Banks comes down out of the pulpit. *You need to be sure, dearly beloved, absolutely sure, Christ died for you. Hello? Somebody? Are you positive, absolutely positive?*

I slip from my pew and walk out of the church. On the sidewalk I think: Jesus himself was a doubter. He questioned the validity of the established religious order. He doubted his ability to do what he was asked to do and, on the cross, he doubted the loyalty of God.

Rather than certainty, I try to cultivate a sense of sacredness. Life is brutal, full of horror and violence. Life is beautiful, full of passion and joy. Both things are true at the same time. The paradox extends to my own being. I think of the words of the Slovenian philosopher Slavoj Žižek, who calls Christianity the religion of Love and Comedy, à la Charlie Chaplin: "The point is not that, due to the limitations of his mortal sinful nature, man cannot ever become fully divine, but that due to the divine spark in him, man cannot become fully man." Abbie, as young as she is, has already felt this dichotomy. On a page of her journal I found this epigram: *I feel like I am someone like God I do not know why.*

I am not able to break with Christianity, no matter how uncomfortable I am with many of its current manifestations. Biblical imagery and Christ's message of forgiveness continue to haunt me, and I know my own redemption lies in Christian tenets, not in others' religious beliefs. But I can interpret the Bible in my own way. I can choose from the creeds that have been passed down; I can make my relationship to God my own, not one that is defined by church doctrine. And I can pray. Of all the gifts Sister Leslie has given me, her Aunt Birdie's Book of Common Prayer has been the most valuable. Thin colored ribbons stick out the bottom. I read Morning Prayer and sometimes Compline. The Compline antiphon is my favorite: *Guide us waking, O Lord, and guard us sleeping, that awake we may watch with Christ and asleep we may rest in peace.*

Since I was a teenager I've lived in a world mostly devoid of divinity. But now I see the sacred includes not just churches but hospitals, highways, costume jewelry, garbage dumps, libraries, the cruising area of public parks. Also pet stores, subway platforms, Ferris wheels, and rainstorms.

From the sidewalk Grace Reformed's brick building looks small and antiquated, like a church stuck in a snow dome. The majority of Grace's parishioners may be more theologically conservative than myself, but my conflict, I see now, was not with any individual church but with church life in general, a life that began at my baptism in that shabby cottage in Sylvan Beach. The *idea* of church still has a grip on my imagination, but I realize now that what I thought was held only inside those walls—grace and divinity—is actually located directly and authentically inside myself. Church is not a set of rules or a specific building but a way of life. My first memories are of my father in cassock and white surplice preaching from the pulpit. My father built his church in Sylvan Beach with his own hands, willing himself and others to create the physical building that would, for a time, house his spiritual work. The act was more important than the structure. My father has always been more a minister of action than a minister of ritual or mysticism. He's trained many of the hospital chaplains around New York City, teaching them to listen to patients' suffering and see them as people rather than as objects of pity. And after two failed marriages, feeling he was destined to end up a loser, alone, he found a way to move on. At sixty-six he married a Baptist minister and grief counselor, creating a new life.

My mother has had a harder time. She sees her years as the wife and mother of a clerical family as tragic, and our relationship has, at times, been an uneasy one. She worries that my house is in a marginal, crime-prone neighborhood and that I'm more interested in writing and other bohemian pursuits than in making the kind of money that would provide my daughter and myself with a stable, comfortable life. I worry that her loss of faith in religion, or in anything else for that matter, makes it hard for her to believe that her life—or my life—can improve.

Much as we differ, though, we have much in common. A few years ago, she heard from my brothers that I'd been laid low again by depression that no prayer or Sunday service could remedy. She called me and talked, for the first time, about our shared genetic history, about the disease that stalked her mother, herself, and now her daughter. "It's not your fault," she said. "It's a hereditary thing. It's just *in* you." And then she said: "I love you. I love you as much as you love Abbie."

One Sunday early in spring, as we walked home together after church, Pat looked at me shyly, uncharacteristically hesitant about saying what was on her mind. "Take me to see that nun of yours," she said. Pat had been unemployed for a while and was behind on her rent. Her landlord was threatening eviction. She'd been asking questions about Sister Leslie for some time and now, in a time of turmoil, she decided she needed to meet her.

A few days later, Pat and I climb onto the 2 train together and head for the Upper West Side. Pat is dressed for the occasion in beige pants and a white blouse. "Other people pray for fifty cents and get seventy-five, I pray for fifty cents and get forty," she says.

At Holy Spirit, Sister Leslie greets us and we settle ourselves in the parlor at the front of the convent. Pat is quiet as Sister Leslie and I talk. When I agreed to bring her, to commingle my two spiritual worlds, it seemed like a good idea. But now as I watch her sit tentatively on the couch, I wonder if I've made a mistake. Pat is silent until Sister Leslie begins to talk about her mother. It's rare for Sister Leslie to unburden herself. She tells us how her mother always felt trapped, how she never really knew who she was and how, later in her life, her depression got so severe that she tried to kill herself.

"Last night I was praying," Sister Leslie continues, "speaking to my mother, when I felt a presence—"

"The holy spirit," Pat says. "You were grasped. God grasped you."

"I know it sounds crazy," Sister Leslie says.

"God communicates with us," Pat says, echoing one of Sister Leslie's own teachings, "in every form and pattern."

Over my many years in Sunday school, I heard some odd theology. That, for example, the dogwood tree was the tree Jesus's cross was hewn out of and that God had punished the dogwood by stunting its growth. Mr. Higgins, who taught shop at the local high school and wore a flannel shirt under his corduroy sport coat, loved to steer his Sunday classes into discussions of Jesus's suffering on the cross. Sitting at the head of a long table, his short-cropped hair slicked back on the sides, Mr. Higgins fell into a kind of trance as he listed the blood-soaked particulars of the crucifixion: how thorns stuck into Jesus's forehead, how the spear made a gash in his side, how nails were driven through his feet. He spoke with the same attention to gory detail that the boys in junior high lavished on their discussions of horror movies. One Sunday, after bearing all I could, I raised my hand. My stutter made me hesitant to speak up outside of church. But this was my turf. I was the minister's kid and I had my own obsessions.

"Why does God make p-people get their f-feet ch-chopped off?" My father and I had visited a diabetic lady who had lost her foot.

Mr. Higgins looked at me skeptically. "Well," he said, "it's God's will."

"It's God's will that p-people get hit by t-trucks and have their f-fingernails ripped off in t-torture?" The children who'd been staring at Mr. Higgins now turned their eyes on me.

"God's will is impossible to understand," he said as he paged through the Sunday school workbook as if there might be an answer inside.

"What about when people get their h-heads ch-chopped off and little b-babies who die from s-starvation?" Around mealtime I heard a lot about starving children in Africa.

Mr. Higgins's face turned from pink to purple. He took out a pen from the plastic holder in his jacket pocket and he wrote a note, folded the paper in half, and told me to take it to my father.

I walked through the church basement, past the curtains that separated the kindergarten classes singing "This Little Gospel Light of Mine," past the confirmation kids conducting a mock trial. I thought: Everyone's always saying suffering makes us better, but why would God want us to suffer if, as my father was always insisting, he loved us so much?

My father was inside his office, his face underlit by a desk lamp. I handed him the note, worried about what it said and worried Dad was going to yell at me. I knew how important it was for my brother David and me to behave and not worry my dad, especially now that my mother didn't come to church.

"What did you do now?"

"I asked why God lets b-bad stuff h-happen?"

"Ah," my father said. "The sixty-four thousand dollar question."

He smiled and got me a square of chocolate from the bottom drawer of his desk. He returned to rehearsing his sermon, his lips moving over the words he'd written on index cards. Earlier I'd heard him preaching into the bathroom mirror, and at breakfast he'd set the cards beside his cereal bowl and read while he ate. Now, at quarter to eleven, he read over his sermon one last time. An organ prelude reverberated through the church. My dad stood. He pulled the alb over his head, put on the white surplice with the belled sleeves, then covered his shoulders with the stole made of gold satin with red crosses embroidered on either end. Last he took the pectoral cross from its hook, placed it over his head, and hung it around his neck.

I walked beside him, down the stairs and through the basement, empty now of children, and into the narthex, where a pimply faced crucifer waited. Ushers in blue jackets with cross lapel pins showed latecomers to the pews in back. With the first notes of the processional hymn, the ushers threw open the wooden doors. The congregation stood and my father stepped into the gap, his robes flowing over the red carpet as he strode down the center aisle toward the cross.

ACKNOWLEDGMENTS

During the completion of this book I had a house fire and my friend Judy Hottensen lent me her home in upstate New York where I finished this manuscript. I am very grateful to her. I want to thank my readers: René Steinke, Susan Wheeler, Rob Sheffield, Rick Moody, Elizabeth Gilbert, Jeff Sharlet, and Jill Eisenstadt. Special thanks goes to the nuns of the Community of the Holy Spirit, the members of Grace Reformed Church, and my family, my mom and dad, my brothers David and Jonathan, and my aunts Bonnie and Sally particularly. I'd also like to thank my assistant Nora O'Connor, my inspirational editor Gillian Blake, and my wonderful agent Sarah Chalfant. I am indebted to the ideas of Saint Augustine, Thomas Merton, Dorothy Day, and Rowan Williams. Finally a giant thanks to my partner Mike Hudson and my daughter Abbie Jones Hornburg.

A NOTE ON THE AUTHOR

Darcey Steinke is the author of four novels, two of which were *New York Times* Notable Books of the Year. Her novel *Suicide Blonde* has been translated into eight languages, and her novel *Milk* has been translated into four. With Rick Moody she edited *Joyful Noise*, a book of essays on the New Testament. Her nonfiction has been featured in *Vogue*, the *Washington Post*, the *Chicago Tribune*, the *Village Voice*, *Spin*, the *Guardian* (London), the *Boston Review*, and the *New York Times Magazine*. A web project, *Blind Spot*, was included in the 2000 Whitney Biennial. She currently teaches in the graduate programs at Columbia University and New School University in New York City and lives in Brooklyn.

A NOTE ON THE TYPE

The text of this book is set in Adobe Caslon, named after the English punch-cutter and type founder William Caslon I (1692–1766). Caslon's rather old-fashioned types were modeled on seventeenth-century Dutch designs, but found wide acceptance throughout the English-speaking world for much of the eighteenth century until being replaced by newer types toward the end of the century. Used in 1776 to print the Declaration of Independence, they were revived in the nineteenth century, and have been popular ever since, particularly among fine printers. There are several digital versions, of which Carol Twombly's Adobe Caslon is one.